FRIED CHICKEN

FRIED CHICKEN

RECIPES FOR THE CRISPY, CRUNCHY, COMFORT-FOOD CLASSIC

REBECCA LANG

PHOTOGRAPHY BY JOHN LEE

TEN SPEED PRESS
Berkeley

Other books by Rebecca Lang
Southern Entertaining for a New Generation
Mary Mac's Tea Room
Quick-Fix Southern
Around the Southern Table

Published in the United States by Ten Speed Press, an imprint
of the Crown Publishing Group, a division of Random House LLC,
a Penguin Random House Company, New York.
www.crownpublishing.com
www.tenspeed.com

Ten Speed Press and the Ten Speed Press colophon are registered
trademarks of Random House LLC.

Library of Congress Cataloging-in-Publication Data
Lang, Rebecca D., 1976-
  Fried chicken : recipes for the crispy, crunchy, comfort-food classic /
Rebecca Lang ; photography by John Lee. — First edition.
     pages cm
  Includes bibliographical references and index.
  1. Cooking (Chicken) 2. Fried food. I. Lee, John (Photographer) II. Title.
  TX750.5.C45L36 2015
  641.6'65—dc23
                              2014042276
Hardcover ISBN: 978-1-60774-724-6
eBook ISBN: 978-1-60774-725-3

Printed in China

Design by Ashley Lima
Food Styling by Lillian Kang
Prop Styling by Ethel Brennan

10 9 8 7 6 5 4 3 2 1

First Edition

FOR MY GRANDMOTHER TOM,
WHO TAUGHT ME THE REAL
GOSPEL OF FRIED CHICKEN

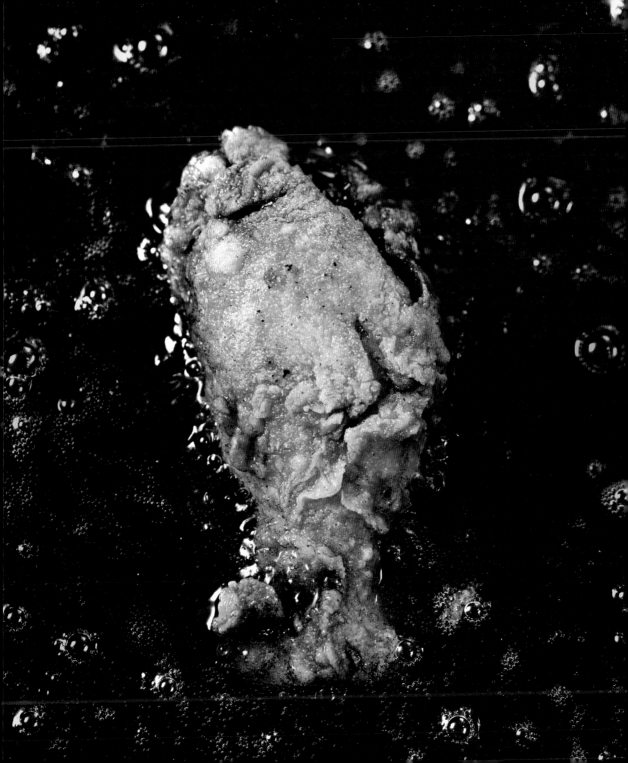

INTRODUCTION

Ask ten different people to brainstorm on the phrase "fried chicken," and you'll get ten different answers. Fried chicken can be comforting or decadent, nostalgic or exhilarating, an everyday staple or special-occasion fare. It can be classic, edgy, spicy, soothing, festive, homespun, extravagant, thrifty—and many things in between. Very few foods are deserving of such wide-ranging and emotional descriptions.

For one thing, nearly everyone has experienced fried chicken at some point in his or her life. Fried chicken is universal—served in almost every country around the globe. Each culture has its own spin on the basic equation—take poultry, fry it in fat until golden and succulent—which means there are countless recipe variations from which to choose.

For me, no food elicits such happy memories as golden, crispy, tender, juicy fried chicken. I grew up in the American South, and in my family, fried chicken was considered a staple, not excess. It wasn't a Sunday if my grandmother Tom's perfectly crisped chicken was not already on the table when we got to her house for our midday meal. It was her cast-iron skillet filled with fried chicken that first taught me how comfort and love could be tasted and shared without saying a word.

For anyone who calls the South home—or even those who merely stopped by for a visit—fried chicken is transporting. It immediately delivers a sense of home, no matter where you eat it. That said, Southerners certainly weren't the first to fry chicken. Name a country and very likely fried chicken is part of its cuisine. I'm convinced I could fry for a lifetime and still discover new ways to prepare fried chicken, one of the world's favorite foods. It's a crunchy and comforting journey, no matter where you choose to start.

THE STORY OF FRIED CHICKEN

Food historians have demonstrated that fried chicken appears in several ancient cuisines from around the world. It seems that as long as chickens have existed, someone was ready to fry them. Though the exact origins of the domesticated chicken are still debated, many historians trace its lineage back thousands and thousands of years. And there are plenty of centuries-old fried chicken traditions, most notably from China, India, the Middle East, Italy, France, and Spain. In other words, fried chicken has been around since long before we started enjoying it in America.

The South undoubtedly has the strongest fried chicken tradition in the United States. Raising chickens was inexpensive and there was no shortage of rendered fat, so fried chicken was naturally found on Southern tables, even in the toughest of times. It was during the nineteenth century that fried chicken was established as a staple on tables across the South.

But even as a staple, the preparation of chicken evolved. Younger birds were used, deep frying became a popular cooking method, and slaves who cooked in Southern kitchens added wonderful spices like curry, which had not been common in the South before the slaves' arrival.

Today, fried chicken still holds its own, seemingly impervious to new cooking fads and food trends. Sure, there are plenty of upscale restaurants doing dressed-up versions of the dish—but there are just as many down-home establishments cooking fried chicken the classic and simple way like I remember it from Tom's table. I love that there are families like mine where fried chicken is a weekly occurrence.

I am a firm believer that fried chicken is here to stay. It is timeless, and a favorite in kitchens around the world. Living, breathing, and eating all things fried chicken to create the recipes in these pages would not only make my grandmother Tom proud, but the process has also opened my eyes and my table to a new realm of the world's favorite food. My hope is that you'll also discover new and exciting flavor combinations, techniques, and serving ideas that will become regulars at your family table for years to come.

FRIED CHICKEN 101

Understanding the basics of frying chicken makes the process much easier and more fun. The information below will tell you everything you need to know to prepare the recipes in this book—from buying a bird to serving it on a plate.

SELECTING A CHICKEN AND WHY SIZE MATTERS

The first step to achieving great fried chicken is choosing the freshest bird you can find. I prefer chickens that are all-natural, antibiotic free, and American Humane Certified, such as Springer Mountain Farms chicken. These chickens are raised locally—at least locally for me—so I know they are treated well and the flavor is superior. These chickens are water chilled, so no chemicals are used in cooling the meat, as can be the case with air-chilled chickens.

When choosing a chicken at the market, reading and understanding labels is easier said than done. Poultry labeling is sometimes vague and can take a bit of energy to decipher. *All-natural* technically means that the chicken was fed no artificial ingredients and was minimally processed. Poultry in the United States cannot be raised with hormones, so every American bird is hormone free. *Free-range* simply means that the chickens have had access to the outside, not necessarily that they ever went outside. *Organic chickens* must be fed organic diets with no genetically modified organisms (GMOs) or pesticides. Organic chickens can be given antibiotics in the first day of life and only later in life if medically necessary. They also must be given access to the outdoors.

If possible, select a chicken that's never been frozen, called *fresh*, because it will be the juiciest and most flavorful. A fresh chicken has never been below 26°F. If the chicken is frozen, the label will always read "keep frozen." Fresh chickens will be labeled as "fresh" or "keep refrigerated." When in doubt, ask your grocer.

The weight of the bird affects nearly every aspect of frying. Larger birds need to be fried at a lower temperature for a little longer than smaller ones. Lowering the temperature ensures the pieces cook through without the outside overbrowning first. For each of the recipes in this book, I've recommended a specific weight of bird, but if yours is a bit larger or smaller, be sure to adjust the cooking time and temperature appropriately.

I recommend that you buy whole chickens and cut them up yourself, because that allows you to ensure that the pieces are similar in size (which makes them cook more evenly). Packages of cut-up chicken most likely contain pieces from several different birds that range in size, often larger than you would have if you cut up your own bird. Store your chicken in the refrigerator, on the lowest shelf possible, to prevent juices from dripping on and contaminating other food.

CUTTING UP A CHICKEN

For most of the recipes in this book, I ask you to cut up the whole chicken into either two, four, eight, or ten pieces. The final product is illustrated on the opposite page.

DO NOT WASH CHICKEN

I know you want to, but don't. Many of us grew up watching our mothers and grandmothers rinsing raw chicken, even tossing it around in the sink before cooking.

Washing chicken was instilled in cooks as much as washing their hands. The USDA has saved us all some time by declaring that washing poultry isn't necessary, and in fact, can create more problems than we think it solves. Some bacteria can be rinsed off of poultry but not all. Rinsing the bird makes it likely that bacteria will splash and splatter in the sink and on the counter, and the chances of cross contamination are much higher than if no rinsing is involved. Rest assured, cooking chicken until it's done will kill bacteria on the surface of a fresh bird.

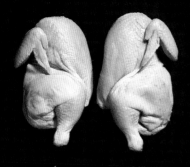

Backbone removed
and cut in half

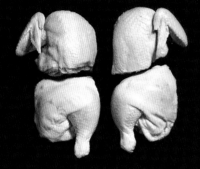

Cut into 4 pieces

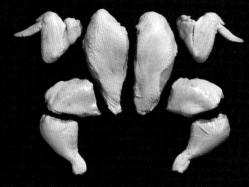

Cut into 8 pieces

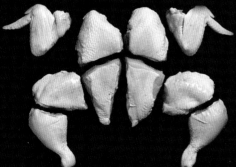

Cut into 10 pieces

THE BENEFITS OF BRINING

Brining simply means submerging the meat in a solution—usually some mixture of salt and water—before cooking it. Brining makes the cooked chicken juicier, because as the chicken soaks in the salted liquid, it absorbs the solution on a cellular level. The shorter the amount of time you have for brining, the saltier the brine needs to be. If you have a long period of time, such as overnight, the solution can be less salty.

BE SAFE

Frying can be incredibly dangerous and you must give it your utmost attention and respect. There are certain guidelines you must follow to make sure your experience is a good one.

Keep a fire extinguisher (Class B or Class K) in the area where you fry.

Wear long sleeves and closed-toe shoes.

When placing chicken (or any item to be fried) in hot oil, lay it in angling away from you, toward the back of the pan. If there is any splash or splatter, it will be in the other direction.

Keep in mind that the more moisture in a food or batter to be fried, the more splattering that will occur.

Do not fry with flammable items near the fryer. Towels, pot holders, and stray aprons should be put away.

Use common sense.

FATS FOR FRYING

You can fry chicken in many different types of fats, but below I've listed the various types that are called for in the recipes in this book.

Oils Vegetable, canola, corn, peanut, pure olive, and other liquid oils are easy to measure and generally good for frying. They are fairly stable and also easy to dispose of once they are cooled. Oils with a low smoke point, such as extra-virgin olive oil and most unrefined oils, are not recommended for frying because they can burn before reaching frying temperature.

Lard This rendered and clarified fat from pork creates a very crisp exterior on fried items and imparts nice flavor. Choose purified and refrigerated lard, since it tastes much fresher than shelf-stable lard. *Leaf lard* comes from the parts of the animal surrounding the kidneys. It's the best lard you can buy for flavor and clarity. I like to order lard from my favorite butcher shop when I need it.

Duck Fat You can buy clarified fat rendered from duck from many specialty grocers or butchers (or you can make your own). It's expensive, but it is very rich and flavorful.

Shortening Hydrogenated vegetable oil has a long shelf life at room temperature, is easy to find in stores, and fries well without readily breaking down. At higher temperatures, shortening is less stable than other oils.

Coconut Oil Nonhydrogenated oil from coconuts is solid below 76°F and melts to a liquid when it's warmer. Refined coconut oil has no coconut flavor, so don't worry about your cooked bird tasting like fruit! Coconut oil comes in small quantities, so it's easy to buy just what you need.

STORING FATS AND OILS

If you don't store your fats and oils properly, they may go bad—and frying chicken in oil that has deteriorated results in chicken that tastes like the oil. Before frying, check the fat to make sure it's fresh. If you've ever smelled a rancid fat, you will always recognize it and it's not something you will need to second-guess.

To keep fats fresh longer, store in a dry, cool, dark place away from heat—so, *not* next to your stove! Buy oils in small amounts to prevent your supply from lingering past its shelf life. If at all possible, start with fresh fats each time you fry (see "Reusing Fats for Frying," page 11).

PROPER OIL TEMPERATURE IS ESSENTIAL

Moisture escapes from chicken the moment it hits hot fat and immediately converts to steam. The steam creates bubbles and that awesome sizzle. But if the meat is overcooked, it loses all its moisture and begins to soak up fat, guaranteeing a greasy, soggy mess.

To avoid this, it is imperative to maintain the oil temperature, hence the need to use a thermometer while frying. If the grease is not hot enough, the steam can't escape and the fat will soak into the meat. As the coating on the chicken crisps, it also creates an insulating crust that is another barrier to grease absorption.

SMOKE POINT

When choosing a fat for frying, it's important to select one that has a smoke point higher than the temperature you need for frying. The smoke points for all the fats used in my recipes are listed below.

The *smoke point* is the temperature where a fat begins to burn and break down into gas (smoke), and it's when the flavor and stability of the fat is dramatically affected. After this point, it's much easier for the fat to ignite, so it's important for many reasons to watch the temperature carefully.

- **CANOLA OIL: 468°F**
- **COCONUT OIL: 350°F**
- **CORN OIL: 410°F**
- **DUCK FAT: 375°F**
- **GHEE: 450 TO 475°F (DEPENDING ON THE PURITY)**
- **LARD, PORK: 375°F**
- **OLIVE OIL, PURE: 410°F**
- **PEANUT OIL: 410°F**
- **VEGETABLE OIL: 450°F**
- **VEGETABLE SHORTENING: 370°F**

DISPOSING OF FATS AND OILS

Leave the fat or oil in your fryer or skillet until it's completely cool. Do not move or transfer hot oil. I return the cooled fat back into the container it came in. Never pour oils or fats down your drain, because they can cause clogs very easily.

You can dispose of a small amount of cooled oil or fat in a container or zip-top bag in the trash, but I like to recycle my cooking oil. Check with a local recycling facility for availability of this service. Or, your favorite restaurant, as in my case, may be willing to recycle it for you.

REUSING FATS FOR FRYING

I remember deeply golden bottles of oil sitting on the bottom shelf of our pantry, labeled "french fries" or "fish" or "chicken." Reusing oil was a necessity then, and it was very common for us to make the most possible of each drop.

I now know that reusing oil even once lowers its stability and smoke point, so I don't recommend reusing it, if at all possible. Your fried chicken will taste better and you'll be glad you made a fresh start.

WHERE TO FRY

I've found that frying outside is the best choice when possible. Even with powerful exhaust fans, when you fry inside the aroma tends to linger for a few days after the meal is over.

If you have a side burner on your grill, a portable electric burner, or a deep fryer, try frying in the open air for a change. You'll need good weather and a stable, solid surface. You also need to follow all the safety precautions, as you would inside. (See "Be Safe," page 8.)

If you can't swing an outdoor fry, it's completely doable inside as well (and you won't get sunburned in the process). A very quick way to keep the cleanup due to spattering to a minimum is to lay sheets of aluminum foil on the counter next to the stove. The foil can be balled up and recycled after you're done, taking the mess with it. If you have a hood, turn it on full blast to help pull the aromas of frying out of the house. Without a hood, you can open the windows and circulate some fresh air.

TIPS FOR FRYING IN BATCHES

If your fryer, skillet, or Dutch oven isn't big enough to fit all your pieces of chicken at the same time without crowding, then you will have to fry in batches. In this case, I recommend you also dredge, coat, batter,

Frying chicken doesn't require much in the way of equipment, and you probably already have most of the tools for cooking the recipes in this book. I recommend the following:

- Asian spider strainer
- Baking sheets, rimmed
- Candy or deep-frying thermometer
- Deep fryer
- Dutch oven
- Kitchen shears for cutting up chicken
- Meat thermometer
- Slotted spoon
- Splatter screen
- Tongs
- 12-inch cast-iron skillet at least 3 inches deep
- Wire racks

shimmy, and shake your pieces in batches. In other words, don't coat the pieces all at once. If a recipe tells you to dredge and then batter and shake, or just batter and shake, do it right before you're ready to transfer the pieces to the frying vessel.

Why? You usually don't want coated chicken to wait before hitting the hot grease; frying should happen as soon after coating as possible. The longer the coating sits, the less crispy the chicken will be when it's done.

INS AND OUTS OF SKILLET FRYING

I was raised on skillet-fried chicken, and many Southerners believe it's the only way to do it. There is less cleanup than with deep frying, and the process is easier to set up, but you do have to pay a bit more attention.

A skillet for frying chicken should be as deep as possible. Ideally, the grease should come at least halfway up the sides of the chicken. The chicken should be placed in the skillet without crowding.

Many lifelong fryers insist on turning the chicken only once in the skillet. I disagree with this practice and find the chicken fries more evenly, with less stress for the cook, if it's turned often. Timing perfectly when the side of the chicken you can't see is done and ready to be flipped is a lot easier said than done.

Many a skillet-fried chicken emerges from the pan with an unmistakable kiss of the iron, that dark spot on the part of the chicken that lay on the bottom of the pan. I tend to like a kiss on my birds, but it's actually caused by grease that's not quite hot enough to bubble and lift the chicken piece off the skillet as it cooks.

You've heard of people who take in stray pets and give them a good home. I'm a woman who never lets a cast-iron skillet go without a kitchen to call its own. If I pass a skillet at a yard sale or an antique store, I always take it home with me. Nothing fries like cast iron, thanks to its ability to hold and distribute heat. Lodge is the only manufacturer of American cast-iron cookware. I own more of their skillets than I can count and don't intend to stop collecting anytime soon.

The ideal skillet size is at least 12 inches in diameter and 3 inches deep. Enameled cast iron, like Le Creuset or Lodge, also holds heat well and fries like a dream. Le Creuset's braiser is a wonderful frying vessel with two handles and the perfect depth.

If you own neither a cast-iron nor an enameled cast-iron skillet, stainless steel is fine, but you need a heavy-gauge skillet. The lighter the weight of the skillet, the less likely it's going to be a good frying pan for you. Never fry in nonstick cookware; most nonstick surfaces can't hold up to the heat.

I also tested recipes in electric skillets. If the skillet has adjustable temperatures that it holds well, it's a worthy addition to your frying arsenal. Electric skillets can regulate the temperature of the oil, so it's easier to fry without constantly monitoring the oil. But some less expensive models don't have a very large or consistent heating element, which results in hot spots. I find that you get what you pay for.

INS AND OUTS OF DEEP FRYING

During the process of frying more chickens than most people can imagine, I fell in love with deep frying. It's twice as energy efficient as roasting in an oven, and you can have deep frying underway fairly quickly. I have deep fried in nearly every contraption and type of pot in existence—including numerous cast-iron Dutch ovens, several stainless Dutch ovens, and my prized Le Creuset enameled cast-iron French oven. These are all good choices for frying. As with skillets, the heavier the pot, the better it is for frying. Ultimately, I find that an electric deep-fat fryer is easiest. I especially like the Waring Pro Rotisserie Turkey Fryer (without the rotisserie unit) that I used for testing these recipes.

Using a fry basket is fun and makes me think of great fast-food fries. If you don't have an electric deep-fat fryer, be sure to buy a good spider skimmer or slotted spoon to help you pull out the fried bird.

INS AND OUTS OF COMBINATION FRYING

Some of the recipes in this book call for precooking the chicken in one form or another before frying it (and in some cases, cooking it *after* frying). Combining some other method—such as smoking, roasting, or simmering—with frying opens the door to entirely new textures, flavors, and aromas. Many combination recipes require less frying time because the chicken was cooked before being fried.

DETERMINING DONENESS

The most frequently asked question about cooking chicken, regardless of the method, is "How do I know if it's done?" I always rely on my meat thermometer. Look for an internal temperature of 160°F for white meat and 165°F for dark meat (and be sure to pierce the chicken piece at the thickest part of the meat). If you don't have a meat thermometer, pierce the chicken and look for clear juices. It's an easy indication. Because dark meat has more moisture than white meat, it takes longer to cook. Depending on the size of the pieces, you can put those in a little earlier than the white or leave them to pull out of the pan last.

DRAINING

There are several options for draining fried chicken when it is removed from its bubbling bath. I almost always place the pieces on a wire rack over a rimmed baking sheet so the hot grease can drip off the meat rather than sit in it.

Folded brown paper grocery bags have been used for generations by Southern grandmothers and many others as a preferred draining medium. Paper bags can pull some grease away from the meat as it sits, but don't try this with fancier wax-coated or plastic bags.

My least favorite choice for draining is paper towels. They do soak up the grease, but the material is so thin that the cooked meat is still in constant contact with the fat.

LEFTOVER FRIED CHICKEN

I like to eat leftover fried chicken just about any way: cold, at room temperature, or warm. If you prefer to warm it in the oven, place the pieces on a wire rack over a rimmed baking sheet to keep the coating from becoming soggy. Warm it in a 350°F oven until heated through.

ABOUT THE INGREDIENTS

Chicken I've found that naturally raised, antibiotic-free chicken has immensely better flavor and quality than other chickens. The better the chicken was fed and cared for, the higher the quality of the meat.

All chickens used in my recipe testing and photos are from Springer Mountain Farms. These birds are 100 percent all-natural vegetarian fed, steroid free, hormone free, and antibiotics free. Not only are these chickens harvested within a short drive from my home, but they are also American Humane Certified. Visit springermountainfarms.com to see whether their product is available near you. If it is not, I encourage you to seek out a local sustainable, natural chicken farmer.

Dairy Products I use whole milk. I also use whole buttermilk. Lowfat buttermilk is much easier to find, but it's worth the extra effort to track down whole because it's so much creamier.

Eggs I use large eggs.

Flour When it comes to flour, I recommend Southern all-purpose flours, like White Lily and Martha White, which have less protein than national brands. This is because they are made from soft winter wheat, which has a low protein content. Look online for Southern flour, or follow the recipe on page 17 to mix up a batch that cooks very much like what Southerners find in any grocery store.

Salt Unless otherwise noted, all salt is iodized table salt.

Seeds and Spices I recommend toasting and grinding your own seeds and spices, which results in a fresher flavor. To do this, toast seeds over medium-low heat in a dry skillet for 2 to 3 minutes, or until aromatic. Grind toasted seeds with a coffee grinder (used only for spices), or in a mortar and pestle. If you opt to use jarred ground spices, make sure they are fresh and aromatic.

SOUTHERN ALL-PURPOSE FLOUR

Store the flour in an airtight container. Check the expiration dates on both the cake flour and the all-purpose flour. Use the earlier date as your expiration date on your new batch of Southern flour. MAKES 1 CUP

½ cup cake flour
½ cup national brand all-purpose flour

Stir cake flour and all-purpose flour together.

SOUTHERN SELF-RISING FLOUR

National brands also make self-rising flour, but, like the all-purpose flour, it is higher in protein than the Southern versions. Self-rising flours have baking powder and salt mixed in. Be sure to read the expiration date on the baking powder can because it makes a big difference. Write this date down to remember when your batch of self-rising flour should be replaced. Store the flour in an airtight container to keep it fresh. MAKES 1 CUP

1 cup Southern all-purpose flour (see recipe above)
1½ teaspoons baking powder
½ teaspoon salt

Stir all-purpose flour, baking powder, and salt together.

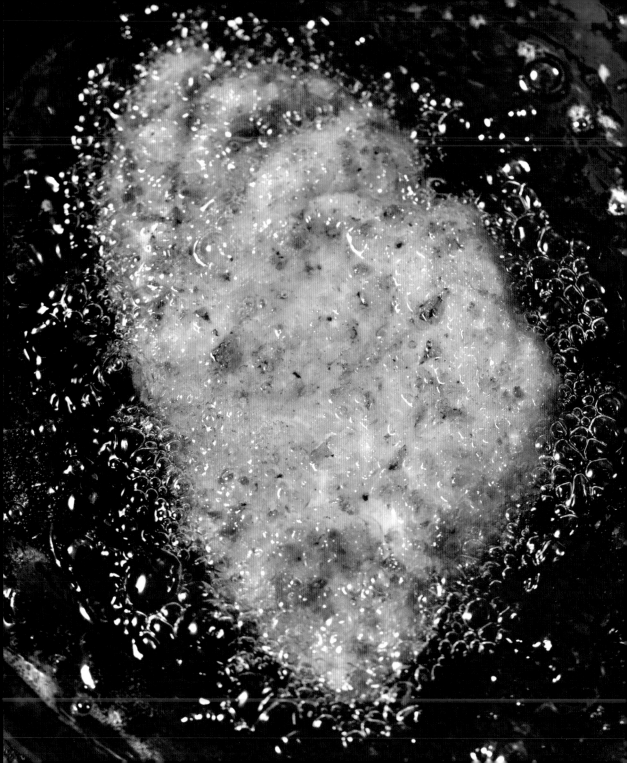

CHAPTER 1
SKILLET FRIED

CORNMEAL-CRUSTED CHICKEN WITH WHITE BARBECUE SAUCE

While living in Birmingham, Alabama, I had my first and eye-opening taste of white barbecue sauce. To first see a barbecue sauce that's on the opposite end of the color spectrum from the typical red varieties is intriguing. Its tart, peppery creaminess is simply wonderful. Common throughout North Alabama, the tangy pale sauce is at its best on chicken, whether fried or grilled. *SERVES 6*

WHITE BARBECUE SAUCE

2 cups mayonnaise

¾ cup apple cider vinegar

1½ tablespoons freshly ground black pepper

1 tablespoon firmly packed light brown sugar

2 tablespoons freshly squeezed lemon juice

½ teaspoon cayenne pepper

1 chicken (about 4 pounds), backbone removed and cut in half (see page 7)

4 cups all-purpose flour

2 teaspoons salt

1 teaspoon freshly ground black pepper

1 cup milk

2 eggs

1 cup finely ground yellow cornmeal

Canola oil, for frying

To make the barbecue sauce, whisk together the mayonnaise, vinegar, pepper, brown sugar, lemon juice, and cayenne pepper. Pour 1½ cups of the sauce into a large zip-top bag. Cover and refrigerate the remaining sauce for serving.

Place the chicken in the bag. Seal the bag, rub to coat the chicken, and refrigerate for 24 hours.

In a 9 by 13-inch casserole dish, whisk together 2 cups of the flour, 1 teaspoon of the salt, and ½ teaspoon of the pepper. In a large bowl, whisk together the milk and eggs. In another 9 by 13-inch casserole dish, whisk together the cornmeal and the remaining 2 cups of flour, 1 teaspoon salt, and ½ teaspoon pepper.

In a large heavy skillet, heat 1¼ inches of canola oil over medium heat to 340°F. Set a wire rack over a rimmed baking sheet.

Remove one chicken half from the zip-top bag, returning the remaining one to the refrigerator. Dredge the chicken in the first flour mixture (without cornmeal), shaking off any excess, then dip it into the egg mixture, and dredge it in the cornmeal mixture. As you dip the chicken in each mixture, lift the wing and leg away from the breast to thoroughly coat all surfaces.

Carefully place the chicken in the hot oil, breast side down. Fry, turning every 5 minutes, for 25 to 27 minutes, or until cooked through and juices run clear. Maintain a frying temperature of 300°F. Drain the chicken on the wire rack. Discarding the marinade, repeat with the remaining chicken.

Serve with the reserved barbecue sauce.

BUTTERMILK-SOAKED, BACON-FRIED CHICKEN IN GRAVY

There are edible staples that are quintessentially Southern and have sustained generations around the table. Buttermilk, bacon, and gravy are certainly included in that repertoire. Serving fried chicken with all of the above takes it to a sacred place. *SERVES 4*

1½ cups buttermilk

2 tablespoons hot sauce, such as Tabasco

1 chicken (about 2 pounds, 8 ounces), cut into 4 pieces (see page 7)

2 cups all-purpose flour

1 teaspoon salt

½ teaspoon freshly ground black pepper

12 ounces bacon, chopped into ½-inch pieces

Vegetable oil, for frying

GRAVY

¼ cup all-purpose flour

2 cups heavy cream

1 tablespoon dry sherry

½ teaspoon salt

To make the marinade, whisk together the buttermilk and hot sauce. Pour into a large zip-top bag and add the chicken. Seal the bag, rub to coat the meat, and refrigerate for 6 hours.

In a bowl, whisk together the flour, salt, and pepper.

In a large heavy skillet, cook the bacon over medium heat until browned and crispy. Using a slotted spoon, remove the bacon from the skillet and drain on a paper towel, reserving drippings in the skillet.

Add enough vegetable oil to the skillet drippings to be 1 inch deep and heat over medium heat to 325°F. Set a wire rack over a rimmed baking sheet.

Remove the chicken from the marinade and dredge in the flour mixture, discarding the marinade.

Carefully place the chicken in the hot oil and fry, turning often, for 20 to 24 minutes, or until cooked through and juices run clear. Maintain a frying temperature of 320°F. Drain the chicken on the wire rack.

To make the gravy, carefully pour off the hot oil, reserving about ¼ cup in the skillet. Keeping the skillet warm over low heat, whisk in the flour, 1 tablespoon at a time, and cook for 1 minute, whisking constantly. Gradually add the heavy cream and cook for 6 minutes, or until creamy. Stir in the sherry and salt and cook for 1 minute.

Serve the gravy over the chicken and top with reserved bacon.

NATHALIE'S FRIED CHICKEN WITH CREAM GRAVY

There are two women who have guided me down the path of fried chicken passion: my grandmother and Nathalie Dupree. Nathalie is my mentor, close friend, cheerleader, confidante, and a driving force in my life. I don't think I would be immersed in the world of food without her. This recipe is from Nathalie's book *Southern Memories*. She covers her chicken so the meat steams from the inside out. And she uses curry or cayenne pepper in her flour, never both. *SERVES 4*

1 chicken (about 2 pounds, 8 ounces), cut into 8 pieces (see page 7)

2 cups buttermilk

Vegetable shortening, for frying

2 cups all-purpose flour

1/2 teaspoons salt

1 1/2 teaspoons freshly ground black pepper

1 teaspoon curry powder, or 1/2 teaspoon cayenne pepper

CREAM GRAVY

1/2 cup all-purpose flour

2 1/2 cups chicken broth, heated

1/3 cup heavy cream

Salt

Freshly ground black pepper

Place the chicken and buttermilk in a large zip-top bag. Seal the bag, rub to coat the chicken, and set aside for 30 minutes.

In a large heavy skillet, heat the shortening over medium heat to 365°F. It should be 1 1/2 inches deep when melted. Set a wire rack over a rimmed baking sheet.

In a bowl, whisk together the flour, 1 teaspoon of the salt, 1 teaspoon of the pepper, and the curry powder.

Remove the chicken from the bag, discarding the buttermilk. Sprinkle the chicken with the remaining 1/2 teaspoon of salt and 1/2 teaspoon of pepper. Dredge the chicken in the flour mixture.

Working in two batches, carefully place the chicken in the hot oil, skin side down. Cover the pan and fry for 10 minutes, checking once after 5 minutes for over-browning. Turn the chicken and cook, uncovered, for 10 to 12 minutes, or until cooked through and juices run clear. Drain the chicken on the wire rack. Repeat with the remaining chicken.

To make the cream gravy, carefully pour off the fat from the pan and set it aside (a clean metal coffee works well for this purpose). Scrape the bottom of the pan to loosen the browned pieces and return 6 tablespoons reserved fat back into the pan. Whisk in the flour and cook over medium heat, whisking constantly, for about 2 minutes. Slowly add the hot broth, bring to a boil, and whisk constantly the sauce is thickened slightly, about 3 minutes. Add the cream and whisk until warmed. Season with salt and pepper to taste, then serve.

SWEET TEA-BRINED FRIED CHICKEN

It's only natural to think that the most popular drink on Southern tables would end up in one of the most popular foods. The sugar in traditional sweet tea adds juiciness to the bird, much like salt does in more typical brines. I use Lipton brand tea, but any iced tea made from black tea will work here. I've added bay leaves, sugar, and salt to make the tea brine even more flavorful and complex. *SERVES 4 TO 6*

8 cups hot water

2 family-size tea bags, strings removed

2 bay leaves

½ cup firmly packed light brown sugar

½ cup kosher salt

4 cups ice

1 chicken (about 3 pounds, 12 ounces), cut into 8 pieces (see page 7)

Vegetable oil, for frying

3 cups Southern all-purpose flour, homemade (page 17) or store-bought (such as White Lily)

1 teaspoon table salt

1 teaspoon freshly ground black pepper

1½ cups milk

1 egg

1 teaspoon cayenne pepper

To make the brine, combine the water, tea bags, bay leaves, sugar, and kosher salt in a large mixing bowl. Stir until the salt and sugar dissolve. Add the ice, leaving in the tea bags. Submerge the chicken, cover, and refrigerate for 4 hours. Remove the chicken from the brine and pat dry with paper towels. Discard the brine and tea bags.

In a large heavy skillet, heat 1 inch of vegetable oil over medium heat to 350°F. Set a wire rack over a rimmed baking sheet.

In one bowl, whisk together 1 cup of the flour, ½ teaspoon of the table salt, and ½ teaspoon of the pepper, and in a separate bowl, the milk and egg. In a large bowl, whisk together the remaining 2 cups of flour, ½ teaspoon of table salt, ½ teaspoon pepper, and the cayenne pepper.

Working with half of the chicken at a time, dredge the pieces in the flour mixture, shaking off any excess, then dip the pieces into the milk mixture, and dredge them in the second flour mixture.

Carefully place the chicken in the hot oil. Fry, turning often, for 14 to 16 minutes, or until golden brown and juices run clear. Maintain a frying temperature of 320°F. Drain the chicken on the wire rack. Repeat with the remaining chicken.

SAGE AND APPLE-BRINED FRIED CHICKEN

When Thanksgiving flavors mingle with crispy salty goodness, a fine fried chicken is created. Each piece is perfectly browned on the outside and just juicy enough to call for an extra napkin. The extremely salty brine shortens the soaking time—and the wait to satisfy cravings! *SERVES 6*

½ cup kosher salt

2½ cups water

1 cup apple juice

1 clove garlic, peeled and smashed

½ cup fresh sage leaves, torn into pieces

½ teaspoon black peppercorns

4 cups ice

1 chicken (about 4 pounds), cut into 8 pieces (see page 7)

Canola oil, for frying

¾ teaspoon salt

½ teaspoon freshly ground black pepper

3 cups all-purpose flour

Fresh sage leaves, for garnish

To make the brine, whisk together the kosher salt, water, apple juice, garlic, sage, and peppercorns in a large saucepan. Bring to a simmer over medium heat, cooking for about 10 minutes, or until the salt is completely dissolved. Remove from the heat and add the ice. Let the brine sit until cooled and the ice is melted, about 10 minutes.

Place the chicken in a large zip-top bag and pour in the cooled brine. Seal the bag and refrigerate for 3 hours. Remove the chicken, rinse and dry the pieces with paper towels, and discard the brine. In a large heavy skillet, heat 1½ inches of canola oil over medium heat to 350°F. Set a wire rack over a rimmed baking sheet.

Sprinkle chicken with ¼ teaspoon of the salt and ¼ teaspoon of the pepper. In a large bowl, whisk together the flour and the remaining ½ teaspoon of salt and ¼ teaspoon of pepper. Dredge half of the chicken in the flour mixture, shaking off any excess. Carefully place the chicken in the hot oil. Fry, turning often, for 16 to 20 minutes, or until cooked through and juices run clear. Maintain a frying temperature of 320°F to 330°F. Drain the chicken on the wire rack. Repeat with the remaining chicken.

For garnish, fry a few fresh sage leaves in the hot oil after removing the last of the chicken. Fry for about 1 minute, or until crispy but still green. Remove with a slotted spoon and drain on the wire rack.

GLUTEN-FREE SOUTHERN BUTTERMILK FRIED CHICKEN

The taste of authentic fried chicken is no longer out of reach for those who want to avoid gluten. Hands down, this is the best gluten-free chicken I have ever tasted, just like the real flour-covered thing! The tapioca starch keeps the coating from being sticky or gummy (as sometimes happens with gluten-free batters). Allowing the chicken to rest before entering the oil ensures the crust adheres and stays crunchy through each bite. *SERVES 6*

1 chicken (about 3 pounds, 12 ounces), cut into 8 pieces (see page 7)

2 cups buttermilk

3½ cups rice flour

2½ teaspoons salt

1½ teaspoons freshly ground black pepper

¾ teaspoon cayenne pepper

2 cups milk

1 egg

⅔ cup tapioca starch

Vegetable oil, for frying

6 sprigs herbs, such as sage, rosemary, and thyme

Place the chicken and buttermilk in a large zip-top bag. Seal the bag and refrigerate for 4 hours.

In one bowl, whisk together 1½ cups of the rice flour, 1½ teaspoons of the salt, 1 teaspoon of the pepper, and the cayenne pepper, and in another bowl, the milk and egg. In a large bowl, whisk together the tapioca starch with the remaining 2 cups of rice flour, 1 teaspoon of salt, and ½ teaspoon of pepper.

Drain the chicken, discarding the buttermilk. Dredge a piece in the rice flour mixture (without tapioca starch), dip into the milk mixture, then dredge in the tapioca starch mixture. Transfer the chicken to a rimmed baking sheet. Repeat with the remaining pieces. Sprinkle about ¼ cup of the remaining tapioca starch mixture over the pieces to ensure that they are thoroughly coated and let them rest for 5 minutes. It will look like there is too much flour mounded on top of the meat. Shake slightly before adding to the oil.

In a large heavy skillet, heat 1 inch of vegetable oil over medium heat to 320°F. Set a wire rack over a clean rimmed baking sheet. Place herb sprigs in the hot oil and fry for 2 minutes. The herbs will spatter in the oil, so stand back. Remove with a slotted spoon and set aside.

Working with half of the chicken at a time, carefully place the pieces in the hot oil. Fry, turning often, for 13 to 15 minutes, or until cooked through and juices run clear. Maintain a frying temperature of 315°F to 325°F. Drain the chicken on the wire rack. Repeat with the remaining pieces. Top the chicken with the crispy herb sprigs before serving.

TANGY FRIED CHICKEN WITH DIJON

Coating the chicken with a generous layer of Dijon mustard yields tender meat and an appealing wavy and textured exterior. Herbes de Provence delivers just a hint of floral fun in each bite. The thicker the Dijon, the better it will adhere to the chicken, so splurge a little and buy the good stuff. *SERVES 4 TO 6*

½ cup Dijon mustard

2 teaspoons herbes de Provence

2 teaspoons salt

1½ teaspoons freshly ground black pepper

1 chicken (about 3 pounds, 12 ounces), cut into 8 pieces (see page 7)

Canola oil, for frying

3 cups all-purpose flour

In a small mixing bowl, whisk together the mustard, herbes de Provence, 1 teaspoon of the salt, and ½ teaspoon of the pepper.

Rub the mustard mixture all over each piece of chicken and let sit on a rimmed baking sheet at room temperature for 30 minutes.

In a large heavy skillet, heat 1½ inches of canola oil over medium heat to 340°F. Set a wire rack over a rimmed baking sheet.

In a shallow bowl, whisk together the flour and the remaining 1 teaspoon of salt and 1 teaspoon of pepper. Working with half of the chicken at a time, dredge the pieces in the flour mixture, shaking off the excess.

Carefully place the chicken in the hot oil. Fry, turning often, for 18 to 24 minutes, or until brown and juices run clear. Maintain a frying temperature of 320°F. Drain the chicken on a wire rack. Repeat with the remaining pieces.

TOM'S FRIED CHICKEN

There is a fried chicken that lives in the soul of each of us, and this is mine. My grandmother Tom could fry chicken without a second thought and never even splatter her Sunday apron. When I need a pick-me-up or a taste of home, this is the recipe I turn to. No matter how many times I make it, it's still not exactly like hers. Simply her presence made it taste better. *SERVES 4 TO 6*

1 chicken (about
3 pounds, 8 ounces),
cut into 10 pieces
(see page 7)

⅓ cup plus 1 tablespoon
salt

1 tablespoon freshly ground
black pepper

4 cups Southern all-
purpose flour, homemade
(page 17) or store-bought
(such as White Lily brand)

Vegetable shortening,
for frying

Place the chicken in a large mixing bowl. Sprinkle with ⅓ cup of the salt and add cold tap water until pieces are submerged. Cover and refrigerate for 4 hours.

Line a rimmed baking sheet with paper towels. Remove the chicken from the salted water and place on the prepared baking sheet. Sprinkle the pieces with 1 teaspoon of the salt and 1 teaspoon of the pepper.

Whisk together the flour and the remaining 2 teaspoons of salt and 2 teaspoons of pepper in a large paper grocery bag.

In a large cast-iron skillet, heat the shortening over medium heat to 350°F. It should be 1½ inches deep when melted. Prepare two rimmed baking sheets with a wire rack on each pan (one will be for the floured pieces and one for the fried chicken).

Working with half of the chicken at a time, dredge the pieces in the flour. Gather the open end of the bag to close and shake vigorously to coat all the meat with flour. Transfer the pieces from the bag to one of the prepared baking sheets. Carefully place the floured chicken in the hot oil. Fry, turning often, for 22 to 24 minutes, or until golden brown and juices run clear. Maintain a frying temperature of 320°F to 325°F. Drain the chicken on the clean wire rack. Repeat with the remaining pieces.

CREOLE CHICKEN AND BUTTERMILK WAFFLES

Most born and bred Southerners have never tasted fried chicken with waffles, though the dish is often thought of as a staple in the South. The combination is an urban version of country Southern food, and while its exact origins are debated, it definitely gained popularity in soul food restaurants in places like Los Angeles and Harlem. Some people say that it's a breakfast food, but a case can be made for eating it between the hours of midnight and 10 a.m., when rich food may be needed to recover from too much fun the night before.

Make the waffles up to one month ahead and store them in the freezer. They reheat very nicely in the toaster, so a late-night craving is one step closer to satisfaction. *SERVES 4 TO 6*

½ cup buttermilk

3 tablespoons hot sauce, such as Tabasco, plus more for serving

1 chicken (about 3 pounds), cut into 10 pieces (see page 7)

1²/₃ cups all-purpose flour

⅓ cup sorghum flour

½ teaspoon salt

¼ teaspoon freshly ground black pepper

2 teaspoons Creole seasoning

Vegetable shortening, for frying

Buttermilk Waffles (recipe follows)

Softened unsalted butter, for serving

Sorghum syrup, for serving

Combine the buttermilk and the hot sauce in a large zip-top bag. Add the chicken, seal the bag, and refrigerate for 3 to 5 hours.

In a large bowl, whisk together the all-purpose flour, sorghum flour, salt, pepper, and Creole seasoning.

In a large heavy skillet, heat shortening over medium heat to 375°F. It should be 1 inch deep when melted. Set a wire rack over a rimmed baking sheet.

Working with half of the chicken at a time, remove the pieces from the buttermilk mixture, dredge in the flour mixture, and carefully place in the hot oil. Fry for 14 to 15 minutes, or until brown and juices run clear. Maintain a frying temperature of 330°F. Drain the chicken on the wire rack. Repeat with the remaining pieces.

Serve the chicken over the warm, buttered waffles. Sprinkle with hot sauce and a generous pour of sorghum syrup.

continued →

BUTTERMILK WAFFLES

MAKES 12 WAFFLES

2 cups all-purpose flour

3 tablespoons sugar

1 teaspoon baking powder

1/2 teaspoon salt

1/4 teaspoon baking soda

2 eggs

3/4 cup buttermilk

3/4 cup milk

1/3 cup unsalted butter, melted

In a large bowl, whisk together the flour, sugar, baking powder, salt, and baking soda, and in another bowl, the eggs, buttermilk, and milk. Add the liquid ingredients to the flour mixture, and whisk until blended. Stir in the melted butter.

Preheat and oil a Belgian-style waffle iron. Cook the batter, in batches, until golden. Cooking times will vary depending on waffle maker.

CHICKEN LUXURIOUS

Chicken doesn't get any more lavish than this version, brined in heavy cream and fried in rich, decadent duck fat. So I say, save up to spend away on this rich and well-appointed fried delicacy. If you really want to take things to the next level, sprinkle some truffle salt over the top just before serving. The breading on this bird has a golden, almost buttery taste. Where duck fat bubbles, good things happen. *SERVES 4*

¾ cup heavy cream

⅓ cup champagne vinegar

2 cloves garlic, smashed

2 bay leaves

3 tablespoons firmly packed light brown sugar

2 teaspoons salt

1 teaspoon freshly ground black pepper

1 chicken (about 2 pounds, 12 ounces), cut into 10 pieces (see page 7)

1½ cups all-purpose flour

½ cup unseasoned dry bread crumbs

2 tablespoons nonfat dry milk powder

Duck fat, for frying

Truffle salt, optional

To make the marinade, whisk together the cream, vinegar, garlic, bay leaves, brown sugar, 1 teaspoon of the salt, and ½ teaspoon of the pepper. Place the chicken in a large zip-top bag and pour in the marinade. Seal the bag and refrigerate for 12 hours.

In a large bowl, whisk together the flour, bread crumbs, milk powder, and the remaining 1 teaspoon of salt and ½ teaspoon of pepper.

In a large heavy skillet, heat the duck fat over medium heat to 350°F. It should be 1½ inches deep when melted. Set a wire rack over a rimmed baking sheet.

Working with half of the chicken at a time, remove the pieces from the marinade and dredge in the flour, shaking off any excess. Discard the marinade.

Carefully place the chicken in the hot oil. Fry, turning often, for 13 to 14 minutes, or until brown and juices run clear. Maintain a frying temperature of 325°F to 335°F. Drain the chicken on the wire rack. Repeat with the remaining pieces.

If desired, sprinkle on truffle salt before serving.

PINEAPPLE CHICKEN WITH PINEAPPLE SALSA

This tropically inspired dish elicits remarks rarely heard about fried chicken; for example, I've heard it called "refreshing," "light," and "delightful." Brining the chicken in pineapple juice delivers a surprising burst of sweetness with each bite. It's one of my favorite recipes in this book. *SERVES 4 TO 6*

1 chicken (about
4 pounds), cut into
10 pieces (see page 7)

4 cups canned pineapple
juice

1/3 cup kosher salt

1 egg

2 1/2 teaspoons table salt

1 (13.5-ounce) can light
coconut milk

1 cup white rice flour

3 cups all-purpose flour

Coconut oil, for frying

Pineapple Salsa (recipe
follows), for serving

Place the chicken pieces in a large zip-top bag.

For the brine, whisk together the pineapple juice and kosher salt. Pour over the chicken, seal the bag, and refrigerate for 8 hours or overnight.

In a bowl, whisk together the egg, 1/2 teaspoon of the table salt, and coconut milk, and in another bowl, the rice flour, all-purpose flour, and the remaining 2 teaspoons of the table salt.

In a large heavy skillet, heat the coconut oil over medium heat to 320°F. It should be 1 inch deep when melted. Set a wire rack over a rimmed baking sheet.

Working with half of the chicken at a time, remove the pieces from the brine and dredge in the flour mixture. Dip the chicken in the coconut milk mixture, allowing excess to drip off. Dredge it again in the flour. Discard the brine.

Carefully place the chicken in the hot oil. Fry, turning often, for 25 to 28 minutes, or until golden brown and juices run clear. Maintain a frying temperature of 315°F. Drain the chicken on the wire rack. Repeat with the remaining pieces.

Serve with the salsa.

continued →

PINEAPPLE SALSA

MAKES 3½ CUPS

1 fresh pineapple (about 3 pounds, 4 ounces), peeled and cored

3 green onions, white and green parts, finely sliced

1 red chile pepper, finely chopped

Zest of 1 lime

⅛ teaspoon salt

Finely chop the pineapple. Stir together the pineapple, onions, chile pepper, zest, and salt. Cover and chill until serving.

PICKLE-BRINED THIGHS

Never throw out the juice left behind in a dill pickle jar. It's a bit like liquid gold, flavored by the pickles and perfectly salty for brining. This recipe delivers juicy meat with a zingy tang encased in a crispy coating. *SERVES 4 TO 6*

10 skin-on, bone-in chicken thighs (about 5 pounds)

2 cups dill pickle brine (juice from a jar)

Vegetable oil, for frying

2 cups buttermilk

2 cups Southern self-rising flour, homemade (page 17) or store-bought (such as White Lily brand)

1 tablespoon pickling spice, finely ground

½ teaspoon salt

½ teaspoon freshly ground black pepper

Combine the chicken thighs and the pickle brine in a large zip-top bag. Seal and refrigerate for 6 hours.

Remove the thighs from the brine and pat them dry with paper towels, discarding the brine.

In a large cast-iron skillet, heat 1½ inches of vegetable oil over medium heat to 325°F. Set a wire rack over a rimmed baking sheet.

Pour the buttermilk into a medium bowl. In a separate large bowl, whisk together the flour, pickling spice, salt, and pepper. Working in batches, dip the chicken in the buttermilk and then dredge in the flour mixture.

Carefully place the chicken in the hot oil. Fry, turning often, for 10 to 14 minutes, or until brown and juices run clear. Maintain a frying temperature of 320°F to 325°F. Drain the pieces on the wire rack. Repeat with the remaining chicken.

REAL SOUTHERN BUTTERMILK FRIED CHICKEN

This is the vision many people have when they think of Southern food, and what a vision it is! Depending on where in the South the chicken is fried, it may be dressed up with tomato gravy. It's optional, but awfully good. You can use a little lard from the fried chicken to start the gravy in style. *SERVES 4*

1³/₄ cups buttermilk

1 tablespoon plus
2 teaspoons salt

1¹/₂ teaspoons freshly
ground black pepper

1 chicken (about 2 pounds,
8 ounces), cut into 10 pieces
(see page 7)

6 cups Southern all-purpose
flour, homemade (page 17)
or store-bought (such as
White Lily brand)

Lard, for frying

Tomato Gravy (recipe
follows), optional

To make the marinade, in a medium bowl, whisk together the buttermilk, 2 teaspoons of the salt, and ¹/₂ teaspoon of the pepper. Place the chicken pieces in a large zip-top bag and pour in the marinade. Seal the bag and refrigerate for 12 hours.

Shake together the flour and the remaining 1 tablespoon of salt and 1 teaspoon of pepper in a large paper grocery bag.

In a large heavy skillet, heat the lard over medium heat to 350°F. It should be 1¹/₂ inches deep when melted. Prepare two rimmed baking sheets with a wire rack on each pan (one will be for the floured chicken and one will be for the fried chicken).

Remove the chicken pieces from zip-top bag and drop them in the bag with the flour. Gather the open end of the bag to close and shake vigorously to coat all the pieces with flour. Transfer the chicken from the bag to one of the prepared baking sheets. Discard the marinade.

Carefully place half of the pieces in the hot lard. Fry, turning often, for 14 to 15 minutes, or until brown and juices run clear. Maintain a frying temperature of 325°F to 340°F. Drain the chicken on the clean wire rack. Repeat with the remaining pieces. Serve with the gravy.

continued ➡

Real Southern Buttermilk Fried Chicken, continued

TOMATO GRAVY

MAKES 1 1/2 CUPS

2 tablespoons lard from fried chicken

1 cup finely chopped sweet onion

2 tablespoons Southern all-purpose flour, homemade (page 17)
or store-bought (such as White Lily brand)

2 cups peeled, seeded, and finely chopped tomato

1/2 teaspoon salt

1 teaspoon fresh thyme leaves, chopped

1/4 teaspoon freshly ground black pepper

1/2 cup milk

Heat the lard in a large heavy skillet over medium heat. Add the onion and cook for 5 minutes, stirring often. Sprinkle the flour over the onion and cook for 3 minutes, stirring constantly.

Add the tomato, salt, thyme, and pepper and cook for about 5 minutes, stirring often.

Add the milk, bring to a simmer, reduce the heat to low, and cook, stirring often, for 2 more minutes, adding more milk if the gravy gets too thick.

GUATEMALAN POLLO

Oregano and citrus are key flavors for Guatemalan fried chicken. Since many people in Guatemala raise chickens, the meat is superfresh and always just a few steps away from the stove. Look for annatto paste, which is sometimes called achiote paste, in Hispanic markets. It stains, so grab an apron. *SERVES 4*

2 tablespoons annatto paste

Zest of 1 lime

1/3 cup freshly squeezed lime juice

1/4 cup freshly squeezed orange juice

3 cloves garlic

1 tablespoon salt

2 tablespoons vegetable oil

2 teaspoons dried Mexican oregano

1 1/2 teaspoons freshly ground black pepper

8 skin-on, bone-in chicken thighs (about 4 pounds)

2 cups all-purpose flour

1 cup finely ground yellow cornmeal

Corn oil, for frying

In a small bowl, combine the annatto paste, lime zest, lime juice, and orange juice, stirring to dissolve the annatto paste. In a bowl, mash together the garlic and 1 teaspoon of the salt, until the garlic forms a paste. Add the annatto mixture, vegetable oil, oregano, and 1/2 teaspoon of the pepper and stir to combine. Add the chicken thighs and toss until well coated. Cover and refrigerate for at least 4 hours and up to overnight.

Remove the thighs from the refrigerator 45 minutes before frying. In a large bowl, whisk together the flour, cornmeal, and the remaining 2 teaspoons of salt and 1 teaspoon of pepper.

In a large heavy skillet, heat 3/4 inch of corn oil over medium-high heat to 350°F. Set a wire rack over a rimmed baking sheet.

Working with half of the thighs at a time, remove from the marinade, and dredge in the flour mixture, shaking off any excess. Discard the marinade. Carefully place the chicken in the hot oil. Fry, turning often, for 16 to 18 minutes, or until golden brown and juices run clear. Drain the chicken on the wire rack. Repeat with the remaining thighs.

BRAZILIAN FRIED CHICKEN

Supposedly the first ruler of Brazil often requested this peasant fried chicken dish, *frango á passarinho*, instead of the royal dishes he was usually offered. Walk into a bar in Brazil for happy hour and the menu will likely include a version of *frango á passarinho*, still popular today.

It is time-consuming to cut a whole chicken into 20 pieces without a cleaver. If you don't have one, heavy-duty kitchen shears will do the job as well. The cuts can be random but some will be straight through the bones. Just make sure the pieces are all about the same size.
SERVES 4 TO 6

6 cloves garlic

Juice of 1 lemon

½ cup chopped white onion

2 tablespoons fresh flat-leaf parsley, plus more for garnish

¼ cup white wine

1 tablespoon olive oil

1 teaspoon salt

1 teaspoon freshly ground black pepper

1 chicken (about 3 pounds, 8 ounces), cut into 16 to 20 pieces

2 cups all-purpose flour

2 tablespoons dried oregano

2 teaspoons baking powder

Vegetable oil, for frying

6 cloves garlic, thinly sliced

To make the marinade, place the garlic in the bowl of a food processor fitted with the metal blade and pulse until minced. Add the lemon juice, onion, parsley, wine, olive oil, salt, and pepper and process until finely chopped. Transfer the marinade to a large mixing bowl, add the chicken pieces, and toss to combine. Cover and refrigerate overnight.

In a small bowl, whisk together the flour, oregano, and baking powder. Remove the chicken from the refrigerator and leave it in the marinade. Add the flour mixture and stir to coat the chicken evenly. Discard any marinade remaining in the bowl.

In a large heavy skillet, heat ½ inch of vegetable oil over medium heat to 365°F. Set a wire rack over a rimmed baking sheet.

Working in batches, carefully place 6 to 8 pieces of chicken in the oil. Fry, turning often, for 8 minutes, or until brown and juices run clear. Maintain a frying temperature of 340°F to 350°F. Drain the chicken on the wire rack. Repeat with the remaining pieces.

After all the meat is fried, turn off the heat. Line a plate with a paper towel. Place the sliced garlic in a metal strainer and slowly lower into the hot oil to fry for 10 to 15 seconds or until lightly browned. Quickly remove the strainer from the oil and drain garlic on the prepared plate.

Serve the chicken sprinkled with garlic and additional chopped parsley.

CHICKEN-FRIED CHICKEN WITH PURPLE HULL RELISH

PURPLE HULL RELISH

3 cups pink-eyed purple hull peas, cooked, drained, and cooled

¾ cup apple cider vinegar

¾ cup diced red bell pepper

1 jalapeño pepper, diced

1 small white onion, diced

2 tablespoons firmly packed light brown sugar

2 tablespoons chopped fresh flat-leaf parsley

½ teaspoon salt

¼ teaspoon freshly ground black pepper

4 boneless, skin-on chicken breasts

¼ cup extra-virgin olive oil

3 tablespoons white balsamic vinegar

4 cloves garlic, minced

1 tablespoon whole-grain prepared mustard

1 teaspoon salt

1 teaspoon freshly ground black pepper

2 cups Southern all-purpose flour, homemade (page 17) or store-bought (such as White Lily brand)

⅛ teaspoon dry mustard

½ teaspoon cayenne pepper

Vegetable oil, for frying

Southerners like to call any pounded meat that's been coated and fried until golden brown "chicken fried." Pink-eyed purple hull peas are a type of cowpea grown across the South and are similar to black-eyed peas, only with a bright purple hull and pink eyes rather than black eyes. This is the pea I was raised on, served with a sauce of sweet stewed tomatoes and vinegar, but you can easily substitute fresh or frozen black-eyed peas (as shown in the photo). *SERVES 4*

To make the relish, in a medium bowl, stir together the peas, vinegar, bell pepper, jalapeño, onion, brown sugar, parsley, salt, and pepper. Cover and refrigerate for at least 2 hours.

Place each chicken breast between two pieces of plastic wrap and gently pound with a mallet until it is evenly ¾ inch thick.

Put the olive oil, vinegar, garlic, prepared mustard, ½ teaspoon of the salt, and ½ teaspoon of the pepper in a large zip-top bag and add the chicken breasts. Seal the bag and refrigerate for 4 to 6 hours.

In a large bowl, whisk together the flour, dry mustard, cayenne pepper, and the remaining ½ teaspoon of salt and ½ teaspoon of pepper.

In a large heavy skillet, heat 1 inch of vegetable oil over medium heat to 325°F. Set a wire rack over a rimmed baking sheet.

Working with 2 chicken breasts at a time, remove from the marinade and immediately dredge in the flour mixture. Discard the marinade. Carefully place the chicken in the hot oil. Fry, turning often, for 14 to 15 minutes, or until golden brown and juices run clear. Maintain an oil temperature of 315°F to 325°F. Drain the pieces on the wire rack. Repeat with the remaining chicken.

Serve with the relish.

CHICKEN MILANESA WITH CHIMICHURRI

Milanesa **is a style of breading and cooking meat that is sometimes called the unofficial dish of Argentina. Often made with steak, Milanesa can also be made with chicken by pounding breast meat, frying it in a skillet, and topping it with a spicy tomato or chimichurri sauce. This recipe is great for beginner fryers. It's quick enough to serve on a weekday night but impressive enough for weekend company.** *SERVES 4*

CHIMICHURRI SAUCE

4 cloves garlic

1½ cups fresh flat-leaf parsley

¼ cup red wine vinegar

1 tablespoon fresh oregano leaves

¼ teaspoon red pepper flakes

1 teaspoon smoked paprika

½ teaspoon salt

½ teaspoon freshly ground black pepper

⅔ cup pure olive oil

2 boneless, skinless chicken breasts

½ teaspoon salt

¼ teaspoon freshly ground black pepper

3 eggs

2 cloves garlic, minced

2 tablespoons chopped fresh flat-leaf parsley

2 teaspoons water

1½ cups unseasoned dry bread crumbs

Pure olive oil, for frying

To make the chimichurri sauce, pulse the garlic in a food processor fitted with the metal blade until it is minced. Add the 1½ cups parsley, vinegar, oregano, red pepper flakes, paprika, salt, and pepper. Process until finely chopped, about 1 minute, scraping down the sides of the bowl as needed. With the processor running, add the olive oil in a slow, steady stream until completely combined. Scrape down the sides of the bowl and pulse 2 or 3 times more. Transfer the sauce to an airtight container and refrigerate until ready to use, or up to 1 day.

Place each chicken breast between two pieces of plastic wrap and gently pound it with a meat mallet until it is evenly ¼ inch thick. Cut each breast in half (as you cut the breast in half, the pounded breast will open up like a book) to make 4 cutlets. Sprinkle each cutlet with the salt and pepper.

In a shallow dish, whisk together the eggs, garlic, 2 tablespoons of parsley, and water.

Place the bread crumbs in another shallow dish.

In a large heavy skillet, heat ¼ inch of pure olive oil over medium heat to 315°F. Set a wire rack over a rimmed baking sheet.

Working with 2 at a time, dip the cutlets in the egg mixture, press them into the bread crumbs to coat evenly on both sides, and then carefully place them in the hot oil. Fry for 4 to 5 minutes on each side, or until cooked through and juices run clear. Drain the chicken on the wire rack. Repeat with the remaining chicken. Serve with the sauce.

SORGHUM PECAN SKILLET CHICKEN

This dish calls for skin-on breasts with no bones, which are somewhat hard to come by, so I recommend asking your butcher to simply remove the bones from skin-on breasts. Sorghum syrup, a Southern favorite for sweetening and adding a deeper flavor than honey, is made from boiling down the juice extracted from the stalks of sorghum cane. Drizzle it over the top of the fried chicken for a sweet note that perfectly complements the savory. Sorghum syrup and pecans have been a favorite Southern pairing for generations. *SERVES 4*

4 boneless, skin-on chicken breasts

2 cups sour cream

Pure olive oil, for frying

2½ cups all-purpose flour

1 cup very finely chopped pecans

2 teaspoons salt

1½ teaspoons freshly ground black pepper

2 teaspoons cayenne pepper

2 eggs, beaten

Sorghum syrup, for serving

Place each chicken breast between two pieces of plastic wrap and use a meat mallet to pound each to ¾ inch thick.

Transfer the chicken to a large zip-top bag and add the sour cream. Seal the bag, rub to coat the chicken, and refrigerate for 4 hours.

In a large heavy skillet, heat ½ inch of olive oil over medium heat to 325°F. Set a wire rack over a rimmed baking sheet.

Place 2 cups of the flour in a bowl. Combine the pecans, the remaining ½ cup of flour, salt, black pepper, and cayenne pepper on a large plate. In another bowl, whisk the eggs.

Working with 2 of the chicken breasts at a time, remove from the sour cream and dredge in the flour. Dip the breasts in the eggs. Lay each piece on the plate with the pecans and cover with the nut and flour mixture. Pat the meat with your fingers to help the pecans adhere.

Carefully place the chicken breasts in the hot oil. Fry for 6 to 7 minutes per side, or until golden brown and juices run clear. Maintain an oil temperature of 310°F to 315°F. Drain the chicken on the wire rack. Repeat with the remaining pieces.

Drizzle with sorghum syrup before serving.

CAMDEN'S FAVORITE CHICKEN FINGERS

As a mother of two, I hear more requests for chicken fingers than any other supper food. I quickly mastered making my own after studying many packages and wincing at the ingredients. Our son, Camden, couldn't be happier, and they're so easy; weeknights will never be the same.

I also like to make another version, replacing the all-purpose flour and bread crumbs with 1 cup of all-purpose flour, 1 cup of whole wheat flour, and 3 tablespoons of milled flaxseeds. It's such a great way to add more nutritious ingredients to a kid favorite. *SERVES 4 TO 6*

2 cups all-purpose flour

1/2 cup unseasoned dry bread crumbs

2 teaspoons salt

1/2 teaspoon freshly ground black pepper

2 cups buttermilk

Pure olive oil, for frying

1 3/4 pounds chicken tenders (about 18 tenders)

Homemade Honey Mustard (recipe follows), for serving

Comeback Sauce (recipe follows), for serving

In a bowl, whisk together the flour, bread crumbs, salt, and pepper. Pour the buttermilk into another bowl.

In a large heavy skillet, heat 1/2 inch of olive oil over medium heat to 325°F. Set a wire rack over a rimmed baking sheet.

Working with half of the chicken tenders at a time, dip them in the buttermilk and dredge in the flour mixture. Stir the flour mixture often to keep the bread crumbs from settling to the bottom of the bowl.

Carefully place the tenders in the hot oil. Fry, turning often, for 8 to 10 minutes, or until golden brown and juices run clear. Maintain an oil temperature of 315°F to 325°F.

Drain the pieces on the wire rack. Repeat with the remaining chicken.

Serve the chicken fingers with honey mustard and sauce.

continued ➡

HOMEMADE HONEY MUSTARD

MAKES ½ CUP

¼ cup yellow mustard

¼ cup honey

½ teaspoon lemon zest

⅛ teaspoon paprika

In a small bowl, whisk together all the ingredients. Cover and store in the refrigerator for up to 1 week.

COMEBACK SAUCE

MAKES 1¼ CUPS

½ cup mayonnaise

¼ cup chili sauce, such as Heinz

2 tablespoons ketchup

1 tablespoon Dijon mustard

3 tablespoon freshly squeezed lemon juice

¼ teaspoon paprika

1½ teaspoons Worcestershire sauce

⅛ teaspoon garlic powder

⅛ teaspoon onion powder

⅛ teaspoon cayenne pepper

In a small bowl, whisk together all the ingredients. Cover and store in the refrigerator for up to 1 week.

CHICKEN KARA-AGE

This Japanese fried chicken is popular in bento boxes, since the chicken is just about as good served cold as it is straight from the wok. The tender and deeply flavored chicken pieces are fried twice for extra crispiness. *Kara-age* is a frying technique used most commonly with chicken, but it's also good for vegetables. *SERVES 4*

3 tablespoons soy sauce

3 tablespoons mirin

2 teaspoons light sesame oil

4 cloves garlic, minced

1 tablespoon finely grated fresh ginger

1½ pounds boneless, skinless chicken thighs, cut into 1-inch pieces

Canola oil, for frying

½ cup potato starch

Lemon wedges, for serving

To make the marinade, combine the soy sauce, mirin, sesame oil, garlic, and ginger in a large zip-top bag and add the chicken. Seal the bag, rub to coat the chicken, and refrigerate overnight.

In a large wok, heat 1½ inches of canola oil over medium heat to 375°F. Prepare two rimmed baking sheets with a wire rack on each pan.

Drain the chicken in a colander and discard the marinade. Transfer the thighs to a mixing bowl, add the potato starch and stir to combine and coat the pieces. They will not be evenly coated.

Carefully place 5 or 6 thighs at a time in the hot oil. Fry for 1 to 1½ minutes or until lightly golden. Drain the chicken on one of the wire racks. Repeat with the remaining chicken, making sure the oil is 375°F each time before adding more.

When all of the chicken has been fried once, fry each batch 45 seconds to 1 minute more, or until golden brown. Drain on the clean wire rack for 2 to 3 minutes. Serve the chicken with lemon wedges.

INDIAN FRIED CHICKEN
WITH CUMIN YOGURT

¼ cup plain whole milk yogurt

¼ cup chickpea flour

1 small onion

6 cloves garlic

1 (1-inch) piece fresh ginger, peeled and grated

1 teaspoon garam masala

½ teaspoon whole cumin, toasted and ground (see page 15)

½ teaspoon whole coriander, toasted and ground (see page 15)

¼ teaspoon cayenne pepper

4 chicken drumsticks

4 skin-on, bone-in chicken thighs

1 teaspoon salt

Ghee, for frying

6 curry leaves

CUMIN YOGURT

1½ cups plain whole milk yogurt

1 tablespoon freshly squeezed lemon juice

1 teaspoon whole cumin, toasted and ground (see page 15)

1 tablespoon chopped fresh cilantro

1 tablespoon chopped fresh mint

½ teaspoon salt

⅛ teaspoon cayenne pepper

Curry leaves are different from the ground curry in your spice cabinet, which is a blend of spices, herbs, and seeds. Curry leaves are small and look like lemon leaves. If you love Indian food, you'll recognize the flavor immediately. Look for them in international markets and store them in the refrigerator. You'll need about 3 (7.5-ounce) jars of Indian-style clarified butter, ghee. Look for it in specialty grocery stores. SERVES 4

To make the marinade, place the yogurt, chickpea flour, half of the onion, 3 cloves of the garlic, ginger, garam masala, cumin, coriander, and cayenne pepper into the bowl of a food processor fitted with the metal blade. Process until thoroughly combined. Lay the chicken in a large shallow baking dish, sprinkle with the salt, and add the marinade. Toss the pieces until well coated. Cover and refrigerate for about 1 hour, turning the chicken 2 or 3 times during chilling.

To make the yogurt sauce, in a small bowl, whisk together the yogurt, lemon juice, cumin, cilantro, mint, salt, and cayenne pepper. Cover and chill until ready to use.

In a large heavy skillet, heat ghee over medium-high heat to 340°F. It should be 1 inch deep when melted. Set a wire rack over a rimmed baking sheet.

Peel off the layers of the remaining half of the onion and add to the hot ghee along with the remaining 3 garlic cloves and curry leaves.

Working in batches, carefully place the chicken in the hot ghee, skin side down. Fry, turning often, for 10 to 13 minutes, or until golden brown and juices run clear. Maintain a frying temperature of 330°F. Drain the chicken on the wire rack. Repeat with the remaining pieces. Discard the onion, garlic, and curry leaves in the ghee after all the chicken is fried. Serve the chicken with the cumin yogurt.

THAI-STYLE DRUMSTICKS WITH SWEET CHILE SAUCE

2 tablespoons minced garlic

1 tablespoon minced, fresh lemongrass, tender white parts only

1 fresh red Thai chile pepper, seeded

1 cup sugar

½ cup unseasoned rice vinegar

½ cup water

1 teaspoon kosher salt

6 cloves garlic, peeled

¼ cup finely chopped cilantro stems, reserve leaves for garnish, if desired

1 tablespoon whole coriander

1 teaspoon white peppercorns

2 teaspoons kosher salt

2 tablespoons oyster sauce

1 tablespoon fish sauce

10 chicken drumsticks

Coconut oil, for frying

1 cup rice flour

1 egg, beaten

One of the most beloved street food dishes in Bangkok is fried chicken, *gai tod*, which is made to order by street vendors with unforgettably bright aromatics. In northern Thailand, it is often served with sticky rice balls, but you can also pair it with regular steamed rice. Wings and thighs are commonly used for *gai tod* as well as drumsticks. SERVES 4 TO 6

To make the chile sauce, in a small saucepan, combine the garlic, lemongrass, chile pepper, sugar, vinegar, water, and salt and bring to a boil over high heat. Lower the heat to a simmer and cook until the sauce reduces to a syrup consistency, about 35 minutes. Transfer to a bowl and cool completely before serving.

To make the marinade, grind together the garlic, cilantro stems, coriander, peppercorns, and 1 teaspoon of the salt in a mortar and pestle until a paste is formed. Transfer the marinade to a large bowl and whisk in the oyster sauce and fish sauce. Add the drumsticks and toss to coat. Cover and refrigerate overnight.

In a large cast-iron skillet, heat coconut oil over medium heat to 350°F. It should be 1 inch deep when melted. Set a wire rack over a rimmed baking sheet.

Remove the drumsticks from the marinade, reserving any remaining marinade.

To make the batter, in a bowl, whisk together the rice flour, egg, and remaining 1 teaspoon of salt. Add any reserved marinade (there will not be much). Pour in about ½ cup water, 2 tablespoons at a time, to create a batter that thinly coats the chicken and easily drips off.

Working in batches, dip the drumsticks in the batter, and carefully place them in the hot oil. Fry for 10 to 12 minutes, or until deeply brown and juices run clear. Maintain a frying temperature of 330°F to 340°F. Drain the chicken on the wire rack. Repeat with the remaining chicken.

Serve the chicken with the chile sauce.

DENISE'S CORN FLAKE CHICKEN

This recipe was contributed by Denise Vivaldo, a dear friend with whom I instantly connected (even though we call different corners of the country home) over fried chicken, a little gossip, canola oil, and wine. Denise still craves her mother's chicken, and this corn flake version stirs up memories of home. *SERVES 4*

1 chicken (about
3 pounds), cut into
8 pieces (see page 7)

1 quart buttermilk

Canola oil, for frying

3 cups all-purpose flour

2 teaspoons salt

2 teaspoons onion powder

1 teaspoon dried thyme

1 teaspoon dried sage

1 teaspoon freshly ground
black pepper

½ teaspoon cayenne
pepper

4 large eggs

¼ cup milk

3 cups corn flakes, coarsely
crushed

Place the chicken and buttermilk in a large zip-top bag. Seal the bag and refrigerate for 2 hours or overnight.

In a large heavy skillet, heat ½ inch of canola oil over medium heat to 325°F. Set a wire rack over a rimmed baking sheet.

In a shallow bowl, whisk together the flour, salt, onion powder, thyme, sage, pepper, and cayenne. In a second bowl, whisk together the eggs and milk. In a third bowl, place the corn flakes.

Remove the chicken from the zip-top bag and pat dry. Dredge the chicken in the flour mixture, shaking off any excess, then dip into egg mixture and dredge it in the cornflakes, pressing the cornflakes to the chicken to coat all sides.

Working in batches, carefully place the pieces in the hot oil. Fry, turning often, for 12 to 15 minutes, being careful not to over-brown the corn flakes, or until golden brown and juices run clear. Maintain a frying temperature of 315°F. Drain the chicken on the wire rack.

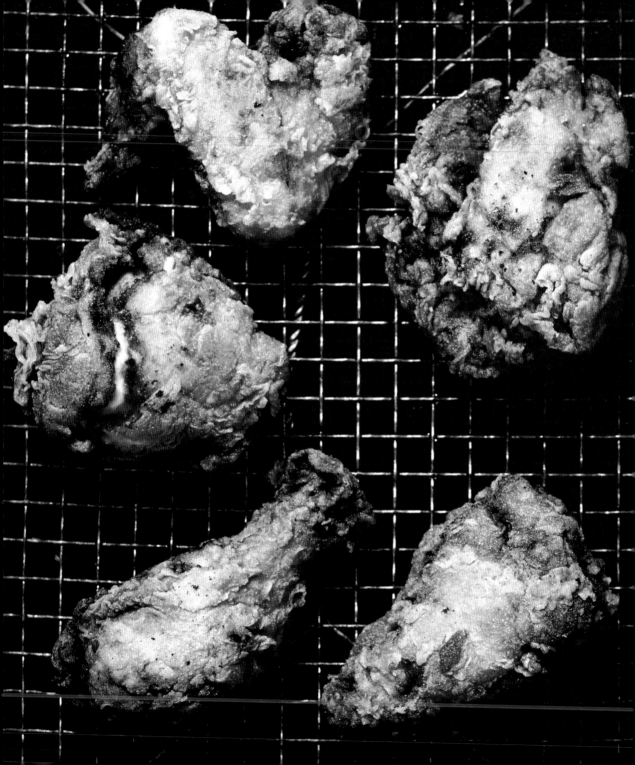

CHAPTER 2
DEEP FRIED

TURKEY-STYLE WHOLE FRIED CHICKEN

Frying an entire chicken is a great party trick, and it saves you the time and effort of cutting up the bird and battering the individual pieces. Most importantly, it yields crackly crispy skin and incredibly moist, tender meat. And since it's a lot easier than submerging a giant, whole turkey in hot oil, you may never fry a turkey again. Carefully measure the depth of the oil to avoid overfilling and splashing any hot oil over the sides. *SERVES 6*

1 chicken (about 5 pounds)

2 tablespoons firmly packed light brown sugar

1 tablespoon paprika

2 teaspoons salt

1 teaspoon celery seed

1 teaspoon chili powder

¾ teaspoon cayenne pepper

½ teaspoon garlic powder

½ teaspoon freshly ground black pepper

⅛ teaspoon ground allspice

Canola oil, for frying

Set a wire rack over a rimmed baking sheet. Pat the chicken dry with paper towels and place it on the rack, breast side up.

In a small bowl, whisk together the brown sugar, paprika, salt, celery seed, chili powder, cayenne pepper, garlic powder, pepper, and allspice. Sprinkle about 1 tablespoon of the spice mixture inside the cavity of the chicken. Coat the outside of the chicken evenly with the remaining spice mixture and refrigerate the chicken, uncovered, for 4 to 5 hours. After chilling, let the chicken stand at room temperature for 1 hour.

In a deep fryer or large, deep stockpot, heat 3 inches of canola oil over high heat to 365°F. Set a clean wire rack over a rimmed baking sheet.

Carefully place the chicken in the hot oil, breast side down. The oil will not cover the chicken entirely. Fry for 15 minutes.

Taking care not to splash the oil, use tongs to turn the chicken breast side up. Fry for 10 minutes longer, maintaining a frying temperature of 340°F to 350°F. Transfer the chicken to the rack to rest for 20 minutes before carving.

CURRIED FRIED CHICKEN

The curry in the coating is just enough to give a hint of one of my favorite spices without being overpowering. Mixing it with cornstarch makes for a light texture with lots of crunch. *SERVES 6*

1 (13.5-ounce) can coconut milk

⅓ cup freshly squeezed lime juice

1 teaspoon salt

1 chicken (about 4 pounds, 12 ounces), cut into 8 pieces (see page 7)

Canola oil, for frying

2 cups all-purpose flour

¼ cup cornstarch

3 tablespoons curry powder

In a medium bowl, whisk together the coconut milk, lime juice, and salt. Place the chicken in a large zip-top bag and pour the coconut milk mixture over the chicken, seal the bag, and refrigerate for 5 hours.

In a deep fryer or large, deep stockpot, heat 3 inches of canola oil over high heat to 350°F. Set a wire rack over a rimmed baking sheet.

In a bowl, whisk together the flour, cornstarch, and curry powder. Remove the chicken pieces from the coconut milk mixture and dredge them in the flour mixture. Discard the milk mixture. When all of the pieces have been coated, carefully place them in the hot oil. Depending on the size of your fryer, you may need to fry in two batches. Fry for 12 to 14 minutes, or until golden brown and juices run clear. Maintain a frying temperature of 330°F to 340°F. Drain the chicken on the wire rack.

DOUBLE-BATTERED FRIED CHICKEN

I first became intrigued with the idea of battering chicken twice while working on a book for Mary Mac's Tea Room in Atlanta. Chicken doesn't get crispier than this and the extra dip makes the crunchiest layer. It's actually best if no one talks during the meal because you won't hear them over the sound of your chewing. *SERVES 4 TO 6*

1 chicken (about 3 pounds, 8 ounces), cut into 8 pieces (see page 7)

1 tablespoon plus 1 teaspoon salt

1¾ teaspoons freshly ground black pepper

Peanut oil, for frying

3 cups all-purpose flour

1 cup water

Arrange the chicken in a single layer on a rimmed baking sheet and sprinkle 1 teaspoon of the salt and ½ teaspoon of the pepper over the chicken. Cover and refrigerate for 3 hours.

In a deep fryer or large, deep stockpot, heat 3 inches of peanut oil over high heat to 355°F. Set a wire rack over a rimmed baking sheet.

In a bowl, whisk together 1 cup of the all-purpose flour, the water, 1 teaspoon of the salt, and ¼ teaspoon of the pepper, and in a separate shallow bowl, the remaining 2 cups of flour, 2 teaspoons of salt, and 1 teaspoon of pepper.

Dip each chicken piece in the wet batter first and then coat with the dry flour. Once all pieces have been coated, carefully place them in the hot oil. Depending on the size of your fryer, you may need to fry in two batches. Since the thick batter can drip, you may want to work very close to the stove to prevent batter dripping on the way to the fryer.

Fry for 18 to 20 minutes, or until golden brown and juices run clear. Maintain a frying temperature of 325°F. Drain the chicken on the wire rack.

RICH CHICKEN

I remember stories about my grandmother adding water to evaporated milk to get by in tough times. I'm sure she would have thought this recipe extravagant, but the ultrarich, silky chicken bath is a luxury that nearly everyone can now afford. *SERVES 4 TO 6*

1 chicken (about 3 pounds, 8 ounces), cut into 8 pieces (see page 7)

1 tablespoon salt

2 tablespoons ground white pepper

1 (12-ounce) can evaporated milk

1 egg

Peanut oil, for frying

3 cups all-purpose flour

Arrange the chicken in a single layer on a rimmed baking sheet and sprinkle the salt and pepper over the pieces. Cover and refrigerate for 12 hours.

In a mixing bowl, whisk together the evaporated milk and egg.

In a deep fryer or large, deep stockpot, heat 3 inches of peanut oil over high heat to 360°F. Set a wire rack over a rimmed baking sheet.

Place the flour in a shallow bowl. Lightly dredge the chicken in the flour, shaking off any excess. Dip the pieces in the evaporated milk mixture, coating them very well, then dredge again in the flour, shaking off any excess. Once all the pieces have been coated, carefully place them in the hot oil. Depending on the size of your fryer, you may need to fry in two batches.

Fry for 12 to 15 minutes, maintaining a frying temperature of 350°F. Drain the chicken on the wire rack.

LEMON FRIED CHICKEN

Our baby girl, Adair, asks for this, her top-choice fried chicken, at least twice a week. Since she's sampled more types than most children will get to know in a lifetime, I think it's a reflection of her good taste. The outside is supercrispy, delivering just enough pucker power starting with the first bite. The meat is lemony and wonderfully juicy. *SERVES 6*

1 cup freshly squeezed lemon juice

1 cup milk

2 tablespoons small capers, packed in brine, drained and coarsely chopped

1¼ teaspoons freshly ground black pepper

1 chicken (about 4 pounds, 8 ounces), cut into 10 pieces (see page 7)

Canola oil, for frying

3 cups all-purpose flour

2 cups buttermilk

1 egg

2 cups panko (Japanese-style bread crumbs)

½ cup finely grated lemon zest (about 8 lemons)

1 teaspoon salt

Combine the lemon juice, milk, capers, and ¼ teaspoon of the pepper in a zip-top bag. Add the chicken, seal the bag, and refrigerate for 3 to 5 hours. Remove the pieces from the lemon juice mixture, drain, and discard the juice.

In a deep fryer or large, deep stockpot, heat 3 inches of canola oil over high heat to 350°F. Set a wire rack over a rimmed baking sheet.

Place 1 cup of the flour in a shallow bowl. In one bowl, whisk together the buttermilk and egg, and in another bowl, the panko, lemon zest, salt, and the remaining 2 cups of flour and 1 teaspoon of pepper.

Dredge each chicken piece in the flour, dip in the buttermilk mixture, and dredge in the panko mixture. Depending on the size of your fryer, you may need to fry in two batches. Once all the pieces have been coated, carefully place the larger ones in the hot oil. Fry for 2 to 3 minutes. Lower the remaining pieces into the hot oil and fry for 12 to 14 more minutes, or until golden brown and juices run clear. Maintain a frying temperature of 330°F to 340°F. Drain the chicken on the wire rack.

BEER-BATTERED CHICKEN SANDWICH

Nearly everyone loves a fried chicken sandwich. This version does not disappoint. Choose a malty ale, such as Bell's Best Brown, or a good seasonal beer from your favorite local brewery. A rich, caramel-kissed brew helps the flavors hold up all the way through frying. This batter is light and airy, similar to tempura. Using two cups of beer leaves you some extra in the bottle, not a bad problem to have—just drink it!
SERVES 6

¼ cup kosher salt

2 tablespoons firmly packed light brown sugar

3 cups water

1 white onion, sliced

2 cups ice

6 boneless, skinless chicken breasts

Peanut oil, for frying

2 cups all-purpose flour

2 teaspoons cayenne pepper

1 teaspoon salt

2 cups brown ale beer

Lime Slaw (recipe follows), for serving

6 sesame seed buns

In a medium saucepan, combine the kosher salt, sugar, and water over medium-low heat and whisk until the salt dissolves. Remove from the heat and stir in the onion and the ice. Place the chicken in a large zip-top bag. Once the brine has cooled and the ice has melted, pour over the chicken, seal the bag, and refrigerate for 5 to 6 hours.

In a deep fryer or large, deep stockpot, heat 3 inches of peanut oil over high heat to 335°F. Prepare two rimmed baking sheets with a wire rack on each pan.

Remove the chicken from the brine, drain, and discard the brine.

In a bowl, whisk together the flour, cayenne pepper, salt, and beer.

Dip all of the chicken pieces in the batter and transfer to one of the prepared baking sheets to allow the excess batter to drip. Depending on the size of your fryer, you may need to fry in two batches. Carefully place the chicken in the hot oil and fry for 10 to 13 minutes, or until golden brown and juices run clear. Maintain a frying temperature of 320°F to 325°F. Drain the chicken on the clean wire rack.

Top the fried chicken with the slaw and serve in the sesame seed buns.

continued ➡

LIME SLAW

MAKES 6½ CUPS

⅓ cup mayonnaise

½ cup white wine vinegar

3 tablespoons Dijon mustard

3 tablespoons sugar

Zest of 1 lime

¼ teaspoon salt

¼ teaspoon freshly ground pepper

6 cups thinly sliced napa cabbage

½ red onion, sliced into thin strips

⅔ cup shredded carrot

2 tablespoons chopped flat-leaf parsley

In a large mixing bowl, whisk together the mayonnaise, vinegar, mustard, sugar, lime zest, salt, and pepper. Add the cabbage, onion, carrot, and parsley to the bowl and toss to coat with the dressing. Serve immediately.

EGG-BATTERED CHICKEN

Like many aspects of frying chicken, adding eggs to the batter sparks debates among diehard fans. The half dozen eggs in this recipe could surely stir the discussion pot. Self-rising flour causes a little puff on the outside while the eggs contribute a nice crunch. Adding garlic to the oil flavors it just enough without being overpowering. *SERVES 4*

1 chicken (about 3 pounds, 4 ounces), cut into 10 pieces (see page 7)

2½ teaspoons salt

½ teaspoon onion powder

2½ teaspoons freshly ground black pepper

½ teaspoon ground mustard

¼ teaspoon ground thyme

Vegetable oil, for frying

4 cloves garlic

6 eggs

4 cups Southern self-rising flour, homemade (page 17) or store-bought (such as White Lily brand)

2 teaspoons celery salt

Arrange the chicken pieces on a rack placed over a rimmed baking sheet. In a small bowl, whisk together 2 teaspoons of the salt, the onion powder, ½ teaspoon of the pepper, the mustard, and thyme. Sprinkle over both sides of the chicken pieces. Chill the chicken, uncovered, for 4 hours.

In a deep fryer or large, deep stockpot, heat 3 inches of vegetable oil over high heat to 350°F. Set a wire rack over a rimmed baking sheet. Add the garlic to the hot oil and cook for about 2 minutes. Remove the garlic from the oil and discard.

To make the batter, in one bowl, whisk together the eggs, the remaining ½ teaspoon of salt, and ½ teaspoon of the pepper, and in another bowl, the flour, the remaining 1½ teaspoons of pepper, and the celery salt.

Dredge the chicken pieces first in the flour mixture, then dip in the egg mixture, allowing the excess to drip off. Dredge the pieces again in the flour mixture.

Depending on the size of your fryer, you may need to fry in two batches. Once all of the chicken has been coated, carefully place the larger pieces in the hot oil. Fry for 2 minutes. Place the remaining pieces in the hot oil and fry for 12 to 14 more minutes, or until cooked through and juices run clear. Maintain a frying temperature of 325°F. Drain the chicken on the wire rack.

HONEYED FRIED CHICKEN WITH HOT HONEY SAUCE AND BISCUITS

A sweet kiss of honey is a wonderful gift to fried chicken. This recipe is a favorite of my children, and they eat it as fast as I can get it on their plates. The herbes de Provence add color to the crispy outside and a floral touch to the flavor. Serve the chicken with biscuits and a generous drizzle of Hot Honey Sauce for a meal that just might become a family favorite in your home, too. *SERVES 6*

3 cups water

2 tablespoons plus
2 teaspoons salt

⅓ cup turbinado sugar

2 cups ice

1 chicken (about
4 pounds, 8 ounces),
cut into 10 pieces
(see page 7)

Vegetable oil, for frying

4 cups all-purpose flour

2 teaspoons freshly ground
black pepper

1 cup half-and-half

⅓ cup honey

1 cup cornstarch

2 tablespoons herbes de
Provence

Buttermilk Biscuits (recipe
follows), for serving

Hot Honey Sauce (recipe
follows), for serving

To make the brine, in a saucepan, combine the water, 2 tablespoons of the salt, and the sugar over medium heat, stirring until the salt and sugar are dissolved. Remove the saucepan from the heat, allow the brine to cool, and add the ice. Place the chicken in a large zip-top bag, pour the brine over it, seal the bag, and refrigerate for 6 hours.

Remove the chicken from the brine and drain, discarding the brine.

In a deep fryer or large, deep stockpot, heat 3 inches vegetable oil over high heat to 340°F. Set a wire rack over a rimmed baking sheet.

In a medium bowl, whisk together 2 cups of the flour, the remaining 2 teaspoons of salt, and the pepper. In a medium bowl, whisk together the half-and-half and honey. In a third large bowl, whisk together the remaining 2 cups of flour, cornstarch, and herbes de Provence.

Dredge each chicken piece in the first flour mixture, dip in the half-and-half mixture, and then dredge in the herbed flour mixture. Depending on the size of your fryer, you may need to fry in two batches. Once all of the pieces have been coated, carefully place the larger ones in the hot oil. Fry for 2½ to 3 minutes. Lower the remaining pieces in the hot oil and fry for 14 more minutes, or until golden brown and juices run clear. Maintain a frying temperature of 325°F to 335°F. Drain the chicken on the wire rack.

Serve with honey sauce and buttermilk biscuits.

continued →

¼ cup vegetable shortening

⅔ cup buttermilk

¼ cup heavy cream

Preheat the oven to 450°F.

Place 1½ cups of the flour in a large bowl. Add the shortening and use your fingers to break it up and distribute it into the flour. Add the buttermilk and heavy cream, stirring just until the flour becomes moist.

Sprinkle about ¼ cup of the flour on the counter to cover your work surface and turn the dough out onto it. Flour your hands and knead the dough 4 or 5 times by folding it over and pressing down with the heels of your hands. Add as much of the remaining flour, 1 tablespoon at a time, as needed to make a smooth dough that is not sticky.

Pat the dough into a ¾-inch-thick disk and cut biscuits out with a 2-inch round cutter, pressing down without twisting the cutter. Combine the dough scraps, pat to ¾ inch thick, and cut into biscuits. Place biscuits, with sides touching, on an ungreased, light metal rimmed baking sheet.

Bake for 16 to 18 minutes, or until lightly browned.

HOT HONEY SAUCE

MAKES ABOUT ¼ CUP

¼ cup honey
1 teaspoon hot sauce, such as Tabasco
¼ teaspoon dried crushed pepper

In a small bowl, whisk together all ingredients. Cover and store at room temperature for up to 1 day.

MEXICAN LIME FRIED CHICKEN TACOS

½ cup freshly squeezed lime juice

1 tablespoon honey

2 chipotle peppers in adobo sauce, chopped

3 green onions, green and white parts, sliced

1 tablespoon ancho chile powder

1 tablespoon plus ½ teaspoon salt

1¼ pounds chicken tenders (about 12 tenders)

Peanut oil, for frying

4 cups all-purpose flour

2 teaspoons ground cumin

2 teaspoons ground coriander

1 (5-ounce) can evaporated milk

1 egg

1 tablespoon adobo sauce

½ teaspoon ground white pepper

½ teaspoon dried oregano

12 (6-inch) corn tortillas

Shredded purple cabbage, for serving

Crumbled Cotija, for serving

Lime wedges, for serving

Sour cream, for serving

Salsa, for serving

Hot sauce, such as Tabasco, for serving

Packed with spices and lime, this chicken is the next best thing to crossing the border for a meal. Each crispy piece screams to become the coveted perfect taco. The batter fries up to be lusciously dark and crunchy. A burst of heat from fresh jalapeños, zip from cilantro, and sweetness from honey add the perfect finish. *SERVES 6*

To make the marinade, in a bowl, whisk together the lime juice, honey, chipotle peppers, green onions, 2 teaspoons of the chile powder, and ½ teaspoon of the salt. Place the chicken in a large zip-top bag, pour the marinade over it, seal the bag, rub to coat the chicken, and refrigerate for 3 hours. Remove the chicken from the marinade and discard the marinade.

In a deep fryer or large, deep stockpot, heat 3 inches of peanut oil over high heat to 350°F. Set a wire rack over a rimmed baking sheet.

In a shallow bowl, whisk together 1 cup of the flour, 1 teaspoon of the cumin, 1 teaspoon of the coriander, the remaining 1 teaspoon of chile powder, and 2 teaspoons of the salt. In a second bowl, whisk together the evaporated milk, egg, and adobo sauce, and in a third bowl, the remaining 3 cups of flour, 1 teaspoon of salt, 1 teaspoon of coriander, and 1 teaspoon of cumin, and the white pepper and oregano. Dredge each chicken tender in the first flour mixture, dip in the evaporated milk mixture, and dredge in the second flour mixture. Depending on the size of your fryer, you may need to fry in two batches. Once all of the tenders have been coated, carefully place them in the hot oil. Fry for 5 to 7 minutes, or until golden brown and juices run clear. Maintain a frying temperature of 330°F to 340°F at all times. Drain the chicken on the wire rack.

Place one tender on each corn tortilla and top with cabbage and cotija. Serve with lime wedges, sour cream, salsa, and hot sauce.

SWEET AND TANGY FRIED CHICKEN

Every now and then I land on a dish with a seemingly magical combination of spice, sugar, and zing—a dish where every bite ignites a spark of pure eating pleasure. I maintain that this is one of those dishes. When I want to bring a tangy, sour note to the flavor party, I like to serve the chicken with spicy pickled okra or pickled cherry peppers on the side. Look for sorghum flour in specialty grocery stores or gluten-free sections of larger markets. *SERVES 6*

4 cups apple juice

1/3 cup kosher salt

2 red chile peppers, sliced

1 white onion, sliced

2 cups ice

1 chicken (about 2 pounds, 12 ounces), cut into 10 pieces (see page 7)

Lard, for frying

2 cups Southern self-rising flour, homemade (page 17) or store-bought (such as White Lily brand)

2/3 cup sorghum flour

1 1/4 teaspoons ground chipotle chile powder

1 teaspoon salt

1/4 teaspoon freshly ground black pepper

1 cup milk

1 egg

To make the brine, in a small saucepan, combine the apple juice and kosher salt, bring to a simmer over medium heat, and cook for about 10 minutes, or until the salt is completely dissolved. Add the chile peppers and onion. Remove the saucepan from the heat and add the ice. Let the brine sit until cooled and the ice has melted, about 10 minutes.

Combine the brine and the chicken in a large bowl, submerging the meat. Cover and chill for 12 hours.

Remove the chicken from the brine and place on a paper towel–lined plate, discarding the brine. In a deep fryer or large, deep stockpot, heat the lard over medium-high heat to 365°F. It should be 3 inches deep when melted. Set a wire rack over a rimmed baking sheet.

In a bowl, whisk together the self-rising flour, sorghum flour, 1 teaspoon of the chile powder, the salt, and pepper and in a second bowl, the milk, egg, and remaining 1/4 teaspoon of chile powder.

Dredge each chicken piece in the flour, dip in the milk mixture, and dredge in the flour again. Once all of the pieces are coated, carefully place them in the hot oil. Depending on the size of your fryer, you may need to fry in two batches. Fry for 13 to 15 minutes, or until dark brown and juices run clear. Maintain a frying temperature of 325°F to 340°F. Drain the chicken on the wire rack.

1 cup freshly squeezed
orange juice

1 tablespoon soy sauce

2 pounds boneless,
skinless chicken breasts,
cut into 1½-inch pieces

ORANGE SAUCE

2 tablespoons vegetable oil

2 tablespoons light
sesame oil

2 tablespoons minced fresh
ginger

4 cloves garlic, minced

3 tablespoons unseasoned
rice vinegar

1½ tablespoons soy sauce

1 cup freshly squeezed
orange juice

¼ cup honey

1 tablespoon cornstarch

Vegetable oil, for frying

1¼ cups cornstarch

¼ cup all-purpose flour

1 teaspoon salt

½ teaspoon ground ginger

⅛ teaspoon cayenne
pepper

Steamed rice, for serving

1 tablespoon sesame seeds,
toasted, for garnish (see
page 15)

2 green onions, green and
white parts, thinly sliced,
for garnish

1 red chile pepper, thinly
sliced, for garnish

HOMEMADE ORANGE CHICKEN

Chinese-style orange chicken is a regular on take-out menus and in grocery store freezer cases, but this bright and fresh homemade recipe is a much improved version of the premade classic. On top of that, it's pretty enough to serve for company and simple enough for weeknights. *SERVES 4*

To make the marinade, combine the orange juice and soy sauce in a large zip-top bag. Add the chicken pieces, seal the bag, and refrigerate for 1½ to 3 hours.

To make the orange sauce, in a heavy stainless-steel skillet, heat the vegetable oil and sesame oil over medium heat. Add the ginger and garlic and sauté for about 45 seconds, or until fragrant and lightly browned. Add the vinegar and soy sauce to the skillet and cook for 1 minute. In a small bowl, whisk together the orange juice, honey, and the 1 tablespoon of cornstarch. Pour the orange juice mixture into the skillet, bring to a boil, lower the heat, and simmer for 2 minutes. Remove the skillet from the heat.

In a deep fryer or large, deep stockpot, heat 3 inches of vegetable oil over high heat to 375°F. Set a wire rack over a rimmed baking sheet.

In a bowl, whisk together the the 1¼ cups of cornstarch, flour, salt, ginger, and cayenne pepper.

Remove the chicken from the zip-top bag and drain in a colander. Working with a few pieces at a time, dredge in the cornstarch mixture. Fry the chicken for 3 to 4 minutes, or until golden brown. Drain pieces on the wire rack.

Warm the orange sauce over low heat. In a large mixing bowl, toss together the fried chicken pieces and the warmed orange sauce.

Serve over steamed rice and garnish with toasted sesame seeds, green onions, and chile pepper slices.

TEMPURA BITES
WITH YUZU SAUCE

Yuzu is a Japanese citrus that has a sour and bright flavor. It is nearly impossible to find fresh yuzus in America, but the juice is readily available in Asian markets. You can substitute 2 tablespoons of freshly squeezed lime juice and 1 tablespoon of freshly squeezed orange juice if the yuzu juice is tough to find. Choose a sake that is very dry to avoid extra sweetness. Gochujang is an extremely flavorful fermented Korean chile paste.

As with all tempuras, serving the chicken immediately is a necessity. Also, wait until right before frying to combine the dry and wet ingredients for the batter. *SERVES 6*

YUZU SAUCE

¾ cup mayonnaise

3 tablespoons yuzu juice

1 tablespoon gochujang

1 tablespoon chopped fresh flat-leaf parsley

1 tablespoon chopped fresh chives

2⅓ pounds boneless skinless chicken breasts

1½ cups cake flour

1½ cups rice flour

¾ teaspoon salt

1 egg

1¼ cups club soda

½ cup sake

Peanut oil, for frying

To make the sauce, in a small bowl, whisk together the mayonnaise, yuzu juice, gochujang, parsley, and chives. Refrigerate in an airtight container until needed, or up to 2 days.

Cut the chicken breasts into 1-inch pieces. In a bowl, whisk together the cake flour, rice flour, and salt. In a small bowl, whisk together the egg, club soda, and sake.

In a deep fryer or large, deep stockpot, heat 3 inches of peanut oil over high heat to 375°F. Set a wire rack over a rimmed baking sheet.

Immediately before frying, pour the club soda mixture into the flour mixture and whisk to combine.

Working with half of the chicken pieces at a time, dip into the batter. Once half of the pieces are battered, carefully place them in the hot oil.

After 1 minute, use a spider or slotted spoon to gently separate the pieces in the hot oil. Fry for 4 to 5 more minutes, or until lightly golden. Maintain a frying temperature of 350°F.

Drain the chicken on the wire rack. Repeat with the remaining pieces.

Serve the chicken immediately with the sauce on the side.

COCA-COLA SLATHERED WINGS

One of my dearest friends in and out of the kitchen, cookbook author Virginia Willis, is praised quite often for her Coca-Cola Glazed Wings. I've never heard of a soul who didn't love them. Eat them once and you're hooked. She broils hers and, of course, I fry these, but either way, they're addictive. Diet Coke just won't do here. Buy the classic. *SERVES 4 TO 6*

1 cup Coca-Cola

¼ cup plus
2 tablespoons freshly
squeezed lime juice

1½ cups firmly packed light
brown sugar

3 jalapeños, finely
chopped, plus 2 jalapeños,
sliced, for serving

3¾ to 4 pounds chicken
wings, wing tips removed
and cut in half at the joint

Vegetable oil, for frying

Zest from 1 lime

2 cups all-purpose flour

1 teaspoon salt

½ teaspoon freshly ground
black pepper

Cilantro, for serving

To make the glaze, bring the Coca-Cola, ¼ cup of the lime juice, the brown sugar, and the chopped jalapeños to a boil in a small saucepan. Decrease the heat to medium-low and simmer until syrupy, about 30 minutes, stirring often. Keep the sauce warm over low heat.

Toss the wings in the remaining 2 tablespoons of lime juice and allow them to marinate for 10 minutes.

In a deep fryer or large, deep stockpot, heat 3 inches of vegetable oil over high heat to 325°F. Set a wire rack over a rimmed baking sheet.

In a bowl, whisk together the zest, flour, salt, and pepper. Toss the wings in the flour mixture, shaking off any excess flour.

Once all the wings are coated, carefully place them in the hot oil. Fry for 10 to 12 minutes or until light brown, maintaining a temperature of 315°F to 325°F.

Drain the chicken on the wire rack.

While they are still warm, transfer the wings to a large mixing bowl and toss them with the Coca-Coca glaze.

Serve with sliced jalapeños and cilantro.

MARTINI-BRINED THIGHS

If you like a dirty martini, you'll love this chicken. Infused overnight with a hefty dose of olive juice, the meat has a salty tang and briny deliciousness. Of course, you'll end up with a jar of olives but no brine, so I suggest using the olives to make your favorite tapenade. Alternatively, refill the jar with vodka or gin for a jump start on your the next cocktail hour. *SERVES 4*

1¾ cups Manzanilla olive brine

4 sprigs rosemary

3 cloves garlic

8 skin-on, bone-in chicken thighs (about 4 pounds)

Peanut oil, for frying

1 cup all-purpose flour

1 cup dark rye flour

Manzanilla olives, for serving

For the brine, in a large bowl, whisk together the olive brine, rosemary, and garlic cloves. Add the chicken thighs and submerge, cover, and refrigerate for 12 hours.

In a deep fryer or large, deep stockpot, heat 3 inches of peanut oil over high heat to 365°F. Set a wire rack over a rimmed baking sheet.

In a shallow bowl, whisk together the all-purpose flour and dark rye flour.

Working with half of the chicken at a time, reach into the bag and turn each thigh over to make sure it's heavily coated with the brine. Remove each thigh from the bag and dredge in the flour. Discard the brine. Carefully place the chicken in the hot oil. Fry for 13 to 15 minutes, or until golden brown and juices run clear. Maintain a frying temperature of 330°F to 350°F. Drain the chicken on the wire rack.

Serve with Manzanilla olives.

CHICKEN WINGS WITH RANCH DIPPING SAUCE

My college roommate smothered almost everything on her plate with ranch dressing, and I still think of her whenever I am within a fork's length of dill. If you love that ranch flavor as she did, you will find these nearly addictive. I think you'll agree my ranch mix is a big improvement over the prepared versions. *SERVES 4 TO 5*

RANCH DIPPING SAUCE

1 cup buttermilk

½ cup sour cream

1 tablespoon dried chives

1 teaspoon dried dill

1 teaspoon salt

⅛ teaspoon garlic powder

3½ pounds chicken wings, wing tips removed and cut in half at the joint

¼ cup dried dill

2 tablespoons dried chives

1 tablespoon salt

2 teaspoons dried parsley

2 teaspoons onion powder

2 teaspoons garlic powder

½ teaspoon freshly ground black pepper

Peanut oil, for frying

2 cups buttermilk

2 cups all-purpose flour

To make the dipping sauce, in a small bowl, whisk together the 1 cup of buttermilk, sour cream, chives, dill, salt, and garlic powder. Refrigerate in an airtight container until needed or up to 2 days.

Set a wire rack over a rimmed baking sheet. Place the chicken wings on the rack.

In a small bowl, whisk together the dill, chives, 1 teaspoon of the salt, parsley, onion powder, garlic powder, and pepper. Transfer 2 tablespoons of the spice mixture to a small bowl and stir in the remaining 2 teaspoons of salt; set aside.

Sprinkle all sides of the wings generously with the remaining spice mixture and refrigerate on the rack, uncovered, for 3 hours.

In a deep fryer or large, deep stockpot, heat 3 inches of peanut oil over high heat to 375°F. Set a wire rack over a rimmed baking sheet.

Pour the 2 cups of buttermilk into a shallow bowl. In a bowl, whisk the reserved spice mixture into the flour.

Dip each chicken wing into the buttermilk and dredge in the flour mixture. Once all are coated, carefully place them in the hot oil. Fry for 5 to 7 minutes, or until golden brown. Maintain a frying temperature of 350°F to 360°F. Drain the wings on the wire rack.

Serve with the dipping sauce on the side.

SAIGON STREET WINGS

If you want a wing you can't put down, this is it. Commonly sold from street vendors in Saigon, these wings have a comforting saltiness that's bursting with umami, thanks to a healthy dose of fish sauce. The garlic is ideal when it's crispy and browned. *SERVES 4 TO 6*

4 pounds chicken wings, wing tips removed and cut in half at the joint

14 cloves garlic

2 teaspoons kosher salt

1 cup fish sauce

1 cup palm sugar, chopped, or firmly packed light brown sugar

¼ cup vegetable oil, plus more for frying

2 cups rice flour

Cilantro, chopped, for serving

Place the wings in a large zip-top bag.

To make the marinade, in a large bowl, smash 10 cloves of the garlic and the salt together until they form a paste. Add the fish sauce, sugar, and ¼ cup of the vegetable oil, and whisk until the sugar dissolves. Pour half of the marinade over the wings in the bag, rub to coat the chicken, seal, and refrigerate overnight. Cover and chill the remaining half of the marinade until you're ready to fry the chicken.

Pour the reserved marinade (the portion that did not touch the chicken) into a small saucepan, bring to a boil, decrease the heat, and simmer until reduced and syrupy, about 35 minutes.

In a deep fryer or large, deep stockpot, heat 3 inches of vegetable oil over high heat to 350°F. Set a wire rack over a rimmed baking sheet.

Place the rice flour in a large bowl. Remove the wings from the zip-top bag, discarding the marinade. Depending on the size of your fryer, you may need to fry in batches. Dredge half of the wings in the rice flour until well coated. Carefully place the chicken in the hot oil. Fry for 10 to 13 minutes, or until golden brown. Maintain an oil temperature of 325°F. Drain the wings on the wire rack. Repeat with the remaining pieces.

After all of the wings have been fried, mince the remaining 4 cloves of garlic and place in a fine-mesh wire strainer. Carefully dip the strainer into the hot oil, just deep enough to submerge the garlic, and cook for 10 to 15 seconds or until lightly browned. Transfer the fried wings to a large bowl, add the cooked marinade, and toss to coat. Transfer the glazed wings to another large bowl and toss with the fried garlic. (Using two bowls prevents the garlic from being coated in the glaze.) Serve with chopped cilantro.

CHINESE LOLLIPOP WINGS

Drumettes are the parts of wings that look like tiny drumsticks. They are perfect for appetizers or tailgating before a big game. Using a paring knife to transform them into the shape of lollipops takes a little time, but it's worth the oohs and aahs from hungry fans. *SERVES 4*

5 cloves garlic, peeled

1 (2-inch) piece fresh ginger, peeled and sliced

1½ teaspoons kosher salt

1 tablespoon hot chile sauce, such as Sriracha

2 tablespoons soy sauce

2 teaspoons light sesame oil

1 egg, beaten

3 tablespoons cornstarch

3 tablespoons all-purpose flour

½ teaspoon ground white pepper

2 pounds chicken drumettes

Peanut oil, for frying

Cilantro, chopped, for serving

To make the marinade, process the garlic and ginger in a food processor fitted with the metal blade until finely chopped. Add the salt, chile sauce, soy sauce, sesame oil, egg, cornstarch, flour, and pepper and pulse twice to combine. Transfer the marinade to a large mixing bowl.

To form the lollipops, grab the exposed bone at the end of each drumette and use a paring knife to push all of the meat to the other end, exposing the bone and forming a rounded lump of meat at one end (to look like a lollipop). The bone should be stripped of all meat to form about a 1-inch stick for the lollipop. Transfer the chicken to the bowl with the marinade, toss to coat, cover, and refrigerate for 1 hour.

In a deep fryer or large, deep stockpot, heat 2 inches of peanut oil over high heat to 350°F. Set a wire rack over a rimmed baking sheet.

Remove the chicken from the marinade and discard the marinade. Carefully place the lollipops in the hot oil. Fry for 6 to 8 minutes, or until golden brown. Maintain a frying temperature of 325°F. Drain the lollipops on the wire rack.

Serve sprinkled with cilantro.

KOREAN-STYLE FRIED CHICKEN WITH GOCHUJANG SAUCE

Korean fried chicken is shaken midfry to remove crispy bits and pieces that Americans treasure on their fried birds. The result is a thin but beautifully brittle coating. A frying basket (think fast-food french fries) makes the shaking process easier, but a wire mesh colander is a good substitute. Gochujang is a fermented Korean chile paste that's almost electric red in color and explodes with flavor. Don't skip the sauce; it's essential. Kimchi is a perfect accompaniment for this flavorful chicken. *SERVES 4 TO 6*

GOCHUJANG SAUCE

4 cloves garlic

1 (1-inch) piece fresh ginger, peeled and coarsely chopped

¼ cup gochujang

¼ cup unseasoned rice vinegar

2 tablespoons soy sauce

2 tablespoons honey

1 tablespoon fish sauce

Canola oil, for frying

4 cups rice flour

2 cups water

4 chicken wings, wing tips removed

4 chicken drumsticks

4 chicken thighs

To make the sauce, pulse the garlic and ginger in a food processor fitted with the metal blade until finely chopped. Add the gochujang, rice vinegar, soy sauce, honey, and fish sauce and pulse just until combined. Pour the sauce into a large mixing bowl and set aside.

In a deep fryer or large, deep stockpot, heat 3 inches of canola oil over high heat to 340°F.

Set a wire rack over a rimmed baking sheet for draining the chicken. Submerge a frying basket in the oil, or place a wire mesh colander nearby. Place a rimmed baking sheet near the fryer. (You'll shake the fried chicken over the baking sheet.)

Put 2 cups of the rice flour in a shallow bowl. In a bowl, stir the remaining 2 cups of rice flour with the water to make a very thin paste.

Dredge the chicken pieces in the flour, then dip them into the flour paste to coat. Once all pieces have been coated, carefully place the chicken in the hot oil. Fry for 10 minutes. Maintain a frying temperature of 340°F.

If using the frying basket, lift it from the oil and vigorously shake the basket over the baking sheet, allowing the crispy bits of batter to fall off. Let the chicken rest in the basket out of the oil for 2 minutes.

continued ➡

If using a colander, use a spider or a slotted spoon to transfer the chicken to the colander and shake vigorously over the baking sheet, allowing the crispy bits of batter to fall off. Let the chicken rest in the colander for 2 minutes.

Check the temperature of the oil; it should remain at 340°F throughout the frying process. Return the shaken, rested chicken to the oil and fry for 10 minutes longer.

Drain the chicken on the wire rack. Add the pieces to the bowl with the sauce and toss to coat evenly with the sauce.

TENNESSEE HOT CHICKEN

1/2 cup plus 3 tablespoons cayenne pepper

1 tablespoon plus 2 teaspoons garlic powder

1 tablespoon onion powder

1 tablespoon plus 2 teaspoons smoked paprika

1 tablespoon chipotle chile powder

1 tablespoon plus 2 teaspoons salt

2 1/4 cups hot sauce, such as Tabasco

8 skin-on, bone-in chicken thighs (about 4 pounds)

Vegetable oil, for frying

5 1/2 cups all-purpose flour

2 cups buttermilk

NASHVILLE HOT SAUCE

2 tablespoons firmly packed light brown sugar

5 tablespoons cayenne pepper

1 teaspoon smoked paprika

1 1/2 teaspoons chipotle chile powder

Dill hamburger pickles, for serving

Sliced white bread, for serving

It's widely known that a few restaurants in Nashville, Tennessee, serve insanely hot and spicy chicken. Rumors of sweating, crying, screaming, and many other kinds of reactions abound. When this chicken hits the hot oil, you'll know immediately that it's got some heat because it's tough to even inhale near the fryer. The pickles cut the heat a little and the white bread is perfect for loading up extra hot sauce. SERVES 4

To make the marinade, whisk 2 tablespoons of the cayenne pepper, 1 tablespoon of the garlic powder, the onion powder, 1 tablespoon of the paprika, the chile powder, 1 1/2 teaspoons of the salt, and 1 cup of the hot sauce in a bowl.

Place the chicken thighs in a large zip-top bag and pour in the marinade. Seal the bag and rub to coat the chicken. Double bag the meat with another large zip-top (the aroma of the marinade is strong), seal, and refrigerate for 12 hours.

In a deep fryer or large, deep stockpot, heat 3 inches of vegetable oil over high heat to 335°F. Set a wire rack over a rimmed baking sheet.

In a bowl, whisk together 1 1/2 cups of the flour, 6 tablespoons of the cayenne pepper, and 1 1/2 teaspoons of the salt. In a separate bowl, whisk together the buttermilk and the remaining 1 1/4 cups of the hot sauce. In a large bowl, whisk together the remaining 4 cups of flour, 3 tablespoons of cayenne pepper, 2 teaspoons of salt, 2 teaspoons of paprika, and 2 teaspoons of garlic powder.

Remove the pieces from the zip-top bag, discarding the marinade.

Dredge each thigh in the first flour mixture, dip in the buttermilk mixture, and dredge in the second flour mixture. Once all thighs have been coated, carefully place them in the hot oil. Depending on the

continued ➡

size of your fryer, you may need to fry in two batches. Fry for 16 to 18 minutes, or until dark brown and juices run clear. Maintain a frying temperature of 325°F to 335°F. Drain the chicken on the wire rack.

To make the hot sauce, carefully ladle ¾ cup of the frying oil into a small heatproof bowl. Whisk in the brown sugar, cayenne pepper, paprika, and chile powder.

Immediately before serving the chicken, liberally brush each thigh with the hot sauce. Stir the sauce after brushing each piece to keep the spices from falling to the bottom.

Serve with pickle slices and white bread.

JERK DRUMSTICKS

Marinating in jerk spices takes days, but the results are well worth a little advance planning. I like to start this recipe midweek to enjoy a fun dinner with friends on the weekend. Then all you need to do is chill the beer and fry the chicken. The marinade has so much seasoning, there's no need to season the flour. *SERVES 5*

2 cloves garlic, peeled

1 cup sliced green onions, green and white parts

1 cup chopped yellow onion

2 habanero peppers

1 tablespoon ground allspice

½ teaspoon cinnamon

3 tablespoons soy sauce

1½ teaspoons salt

1 teaspoon freshly ground black pepper

1 teaspoon sugar

¼ cup freshly squeezed lime juice

1 teaspoon dried thyme leaves

3 pounds chicken drumsticks

Peanut oil, for frying

3 cups coconut flour

Pulse the garlic in the bowl of a food processor fitted with the metal blade until finely minced. Add the onions and peppers and pulse until finely chopped. Add the allspice, cinnamon, soy sauce, salt, pepper, sugar, lime juice, and thyme and process until combined. Pour the marinade into a large zip-top bag and add the drumsticks. Seal the bag and rub to coat the chicken. Double bag the chicken with another large zip-top (the aroma of the marinade is strong). Seal and refrigerate for 2 to 3 days.

In a deep fryer or large, deep stockpot, heat 3 inches of peanut oil over high heat to 350°F. Set a wire rack over a rimmed baking sheet.

Remove the drumsticks from the marinade but do not rinse the marinade off. Discard the remaining marinade. Place the coconut flour in a large mixing bowl, add 1 drumstick at a time, and toss to coat well. Repeat with the remaining chicken.

Carefully place the drumsticks in the hot oil. Fry for 8 to 10 minutes, or until dark brown and juices run clear. Maintain a frying temperature of 340°F. Drain the chicken on the wire rack.

FRIED CHICKEN SKINS WITH LIME MUSTARD DRIZZLE

This is the perfect bar snack to savor with a glass of Champagne or a cold beer. (Even top sommeliers will tell you that fried foods and bubbly are a match made in heaven.) Cornstarch added to the flour creates an airy crunch in every light, salty bite. It's almost impossible to eat only one!

Ask your butcher for chicken skins, or pull them from chicken pieces and reserve the meat for another use. Kitchen shears make easy work of cutting the skins into pieces. *SERVES 4 TO 6*

1 cup buttermilk

1/2 teaspoon cayenne pepper

12 ounces chicken skins, cut into approximately 3-inch pieces

LIME MUSTARD DRIZZLE

1/4 cup honey

1 tablespoon whole-grain mustard

Zest of 1 lime

Canola oil, for frying

1 cup all-purpose flour

1 cup cornstarch

1 1/2 teaspoons salt

1/2 teaspoon freshly ground black pepper

Combine the buttermilk and cayenne pepper in a large zip-top bag. Add the chicken skins, seal the bag, and refrigerate for 4 to 6 hours.

To make the drizzle, in a small bowl, whisk together the honey, mustard, and lime zest. Cover and set aside.

In a deep fryer or large, deep stockpot, heat 3 inches of canola oil over high heat to 375°F. Set a wire rack over a rimmed baking sheet.

Stir together the flour, cornstarch, salt, and pepper in a bowl.

Drain the chicken skins, discarding the marinade. Dredge the skins in the flour mixture.

Carefully place them in the hot oil and fry for 3 to 5 minutes, or until puffed and light golden brown. Maintain a frying temperature of 325°F. Use a slotted spoon and gently stir the skins in the oil twice, then drain them on the wire rack.

Arrange the chicken skins on a platter and pour 2 tablespoons of the drizzle over them. Serve the remaining drizzle on the side for dipping.

CHAPTER 3
COMBINATION FRIED

INDONESIAN FRIED CHICKEN

Ayam goreng kremes, **the fried chicken of Indonesia and Southeast Asia, is a hugely popular street food. The clever cooking technique starts with poaching the chicken and then frying it. With no coating on the outside, the supercrunch comes from frying flour-thickened drops of the poaching liquid to make little crunchy pieces. They are piled on each piece of chicken to make little crispy mounds.** *SERVES 4*

6 cloves garlic, peeled

4 candlenuts or Brazil nuts

1 shallot, peeled

1 (2-inch) piece fresh turmeric, peeled and sliced

1 (2-inch) piece fresh ginger, peeled and sliced

1 tablespoon whole coriander

1 tablespoon palm sugar

2 teaspoons kosher salt

1 chicken (about 3 pounds), cut into 8 pieces (see page 7)

1 (2-inch) piece lemongrass, tough outer leaves removed and finely chopped

2¼ cups unsweetened coconut water

¼ cup plus 2 tablespoons rice flour

¼ cup plus 2 tablespoons all-purpose flour

Coconut oil, for frying

To make the marinade, grind the garlic, nuts, shallot, turmeric, ginger, coriander, palm sugar, and salt using a mortar and pestle. Transfer the mixture to a large bowl, add the chicken pieces, and toss to coat. Cover and refrigerate for 2 hours.

Transfer the chicken and marinade to a large Dutch oven. Add the lemongrass, coconut water, and enough water just to cover the chicken. Bring to a boil. Decrease the heat and simmer for 15 minutes, turning the chicken once. Remove the meat from the Dutch oven and set aside. Continue to simmer the liquid for 5 more minutes.

Transfer 2 cups of the cooking liquid to a medium bowl, add the rice flour and the all-purpose flour, whisk to combine, and set aside.

In a large wok, heat the coconut oil over medium-high heat to 360°F. It should be 2 inches deep when melted. Set a wire rack over a rimmed baking sheet.

Working in batches, place the chicken into the hot oil and fry for 6 minutes, turning often. Drain the pieces on the wire rack. Repeat with the remaining chicken, making sure the oil reaches 360°F each time before adding more pieces.

After all of the chicken is fried, decrease the heat and allow the oil to cool to about 320°F. Gently pour ½ cup of the thickened cooking liquid into the oil and fry for 6 to 8 minutes, or until crispy and brown. It will bubble and splatter a lot. Using a spider or a wire strainer, transfer the crunchy pieces to a paper towel–lined plate and repeat with remaining batter.

Serve the chicken topped with the crunchy pieces.

CHICKEN COUNTRY CAPTAIN

1/3 cup unsalted butter

1/3 cup pure olive oil

1 chicken (about
2 pounds, 8 ounces),
cut into 10 pieces
(see page 7)

1 large yellow onion,
chopped

1 large green bell pepper,
chopped

2 cloves garlic, minced

2 to 3 teaspoons curry
powder

1 Granny Smith apple,
cored and diced

2 pounds tomatoes, peeled,
seeded, and chopped

1 teaspoon turbinado sugar

1 cup currants

3/4 teaspoon salt

1 tablespoon chopped fresh
flat-leaf parsley

4 cups cooked rice

1/2 cup flaked unsweetened
coconut, for serving

1/2 cup toasted peanuts
or almonds, for serving

1/2 cup Major Grey's or
similar chutney, for serving

This recipe is from my dear friend Damon Lee Fowler, author and immensely talented authority on Southern food history. Country Captain is an extremely flavorful and comforting combination of saucy chicken, curry, and tomatoes served over rice. It's been popular on the Atlantic coast since the nineteenth century. Where it originated remains debatable, but it's most likely an English adaptation of Indian cookery that came to America via Britain's East Indian spice and tea trade. Major Grey's chutney is made with mangoes and is common in the condiment section of most grocery stores. If tomatoes aren't in season, substitute 2 cups of the canned Italian variety, chopping them before using. Choose the curry amount that's best for your taste. *SERVES 4*

In a large heavy skillet with a lid, heat the butter and oil over medium-high heat until sizzling. Working with half of the chicken at a time, carefully place the pieces in the hot oil and fry for about 4 minutes per side, or until golden brown.

Carefully pour off the hot oil and butter, reserving about 3 tablespoons in the skillet. Add the onion and the green pepper. Cook, stirring frequently, until softened, about 5 minutes. Add the garlic and the curry and cook for 1 minute, or until fragrant.

Add the apple and toss until it is coated with the curry. Add the tomatoes, sugar, and currants and bring to a boil. Return the chicken to the skillet and sprinkle with salt. Turn each piece so it is well coated with the sauce. Decrease the heat to low and cover. Simmer gently, turning the chicken occasionally, for 30 minutes, or until very tender.

Remove the pieces to a warm platter. If the sauce is thinner than you would like, raise the heat to medium-high and simmer until thickened. Remove the skillet from the heat, stir in the parsley, and pour the sauce over the chicken.

Serve with the rice, passing the coconut, peanuts, and chutney at the table.

ROASTED AND FRIED CHICKEN

Baking the bird before frying it allows for a shorter frying time and a simple guarantee that each piece will be evenly cooked through. Soaking in highly acidic sour cream and buttermilk makes each bite tangy under the crunch of the cornmeal crust. *SERVES 4 TO 6*

2 cups sour cream

2 cups buttermilk

1 chicken (about 3 pounds, 12 ounces), cut into 10 pieces (see page 7)

1 tablespoon olive oil

1¼ teaspoons salt

1 teaspoon freshly ground black pepper

1½ cups Southern all-purpose flour, homemade (page 17) or store-bought (such as White Lily brand)

½ cup finely ground yellow cornmeal

Peanut oil, for frying

Stir together the sour cream and 1 cup of the buttermilk and pour into a large zip-top bag. Add the chicken, seal the bag, rub to coat the chicken, and refrigerate for 12 hours.

Preheat the oven to 400°F. Remove the chicken from the zip-top bag, rinse the pieces, and pat them dry with paper towels. Arrange the chicken on a rimmed baking sheet. Rub the meat with olive oil and sprinkle with ½ teaspoon of the salt and ¼ teaspoon of the pepper. Bake for 20 minutes. Remove the chicken from the oven and cool for about 20 minutes.

In a large bowl, whisk together the flour, cornmeal, and the remaining ¾ teaspoon of salt and ¾ teaspoon of pepper.

In a large heavy skillet, heat 1 inch of peanut oil over medium heat to 360°F. Set a wire rack over a rimmed baking sheet.

Working with half of the chicken at a time, dip the pieces into the remaining 1 cup of buttermilk and dredge in the flour mixture. Carefully place the chicken in the hot oil. Fry for 8 to 10 minutes, or until golden brown and juices run clear, turning frequently. Maintain a frying temperature of 330°F. Drain the chicken on the wire rack. Repeat with the remaining chicken.

LATIN FRIED CHICKEN WITH SMOKY KETCHUP

My friend Sandra Gutierrez cleverly fries her spiced chicken and then finishes it off in a hot oven. The chicken is moist with not a hint of grease. She serves it with her Smoky Ketchup, adding a gutsy kick of heat you'll want to serve on nearly everything. *SERVES 6*

SMOKY KETCHUP

1½ cups ketchup

1 large chipotle chile in adobo, chopped to a fine paste

1 teaspoon adobo sauce

2 teaspoons ancho chile powder

1½ cups buttermilk

¼ cup chopped fresh cilantro

1 large chipotle chile in adobo sauce, minced

1 teaspoon adobo sauce

1½ teaspoons garlic powder

2½ teaspoons salt

¾ teaspoon freshly ground black pepper

1 chicken (about 5 pounds), cut into 10 pieces (see page 7)

3 cups Southern self-rising flour, homemade (page 17) or store-bought (such as White Lily brand)

2 teaspoons paprika

1 teaspoon ground coriander

1 teaspoon cayenne pepper

1 teaspoon ancho chile powder

Vegetable oil, for frying

To make the smoky ketchup, in a small bowl, whisk together the ketchup, chipotle, adobo sauce, and chile powder. Cover and chill until ready to use. The ketchup will keep, covered tightly, for up to 1 week in the refrigerator.

In a bowl, whisk together the buttermilk, cilantro, chipotle, adobo sauce, ½ teaspoon of the garlic powder, 1 teaspoon of the salt, and ¼ teaspoon of the pepper. Place the chicken in a large zip-top bag and pour the buttermilk mixture over it. Seal the bag, rub to coat the meat, and refrigerate for 6 to 12 hours.

Preheat the oven to 325°F. Prepare two rimmed baking sheets with a wire rack on each pan.

In a large bowl, whisk together the flour, paprika, coriander, cayenne pepper, chile powder, and the remaining 1½ teaspoons of salt, 1 teaspoon of garlic powder, and ½ teaspoon of pepper. Dredge the chicken in the flour mixture and lay on one of the prepared baking sheets, allowing it to set for 5 minutes.

In a deep fryer or large, deep stockpot, heat 3½ inches of vegetable oil over high heat to 360°F.

Working in batches, dredge the chicken in the flour mixture a second time. Carefully place the pieces in the hot oil and fry for 8 to 10 minutes, or until the crust is crispy and reddish brown.

Transfer the fried chicken to the other prepared rack and bake for 20 to 25 minutes, or until cooked through and juices run clear.

SMOKED AND FRIED CHICKEN

It's unusual to enjoy a smoky, rich flavor inside a crispy, crunchy coating, but with this two-step recipe, you can savor both. The chicken is browned inside and out thanks to smoke penetrating all the way to the bone. SERVES 4 TO 6

1 chicken (about 3 pounds, 12 ounces), cut into 10 pieces (see page 7)

2 cups plain whole milk yogurt

2½ cups hickory wood chips, soaked in water overnight, for smoking

3 cups Southern self-rising flour, homemade (page 17) or store-bought (such as White Lily brand)

1½ teaspoons salt

1½ teaspoons freshly ground black pepper

Peanut oil, for frying

3 cups buttermilk

Combine the chicken pieces and the yogurt in a large zip-top bag. Seal the bag, rub to coat the meat, and refrigerate for 12 hours.

Light natural charcoal in a smoker (such as a Big Green Egg). Bring the internal temperature of the smoker to 250°F. Maintain the temperature of the smoker for about 15 minutes. Drain the wood chips and place directly on the hot coals.

Remove the chicken from the zip-top bag, discarding the yogurt, but do not rinse the marinade off of the chicken. Place the pieces directly on the grate of the smoker and smoke for 30 minutes, maintaining a temperature of 250°F. Remove the chicken from the smoker (the meat will be brown).

In a bowl, whisk together the flour, salt, and pepper.

In a 12-inch cast-iron skillet, heat 1 inch of peanut oil over medium heat to 360°F. Set a wire rack over a rimmed baking sheet.

Working with half of the chicken at a time, dredge in the flour mixture, dip into the buttermilk, then dredge in the flour mixture again. Carefully place the chicken in the hot oil. Fry for 10 to 12 minutes, or until golden brown and juices run clear, turning frequently. Maintain a frying temperature of 330°F to 340°F. Drain the chicken on the wire rack. Repeat with the remaining pieces.

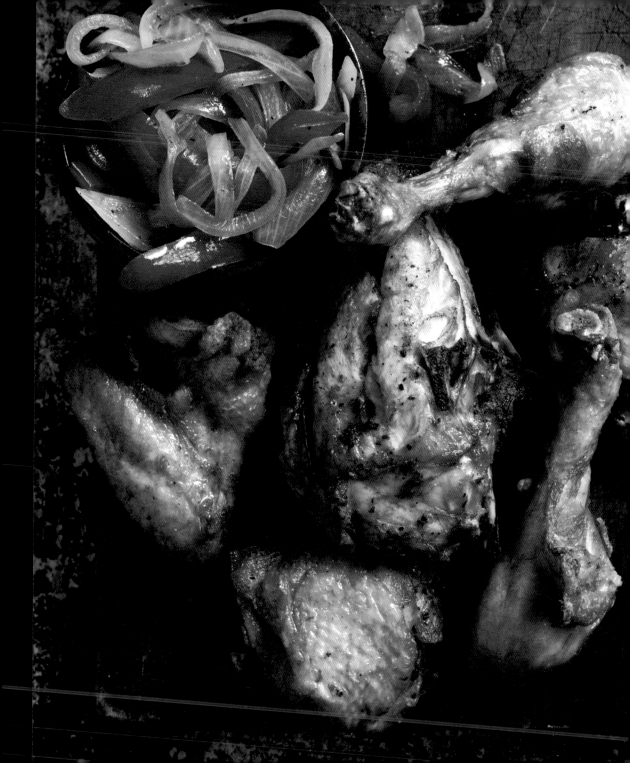

WEST AFRICAN FRIED CHICKEN WITH SAUTÉED ONIONS AND PEPPERS

Throughout much of West Africa, chicken is considered special-occasion fare. Serving the chicken with the traditional marinated onions and colorful peppers makes the dish as pretty as it is good. Bouillon cubes are a replacement for *sumbala*, a paste-like condiment common in West Africa. Look for the peppery and citrusy grains of paradise in international markets or specialty spice stores, or order it online. *SERVES 4*

1 tablespoon grains of paradise

1 or 2 Scotch bonnet peppers, finely chopped

1 small onion, diced

2 cloves garlic, minced

1 (1-inch) piece fresh ginger, peeled and grated

2 beef bouillon cubes

1 tablespoon paprika

2 teaspoons kosher salt

2 tablespoon vegetable oil, plus more for frying

1 chicken (about 4 pounds), cut into 10 pieces (see page 7)

1 large onion, sliced

1 large red bell pepper, cored, seeded, and cut into ½-inch strips

To make the marinade, grind the grains of paradise in a mortar and pestle. Add the Scotch bonnet peppers (use 1 if you want less heat, 2 if you want more), onion, garlic, ginger, bouillon cubes, paprika, and salt, grinding to combine. Transfer to a small bowl and stir in 1 tablespoon of the vegetable oil.

Place the chicken in large zip-top bag and add about three-fourths of the marinade. Seal the bag and rub to coat the chicken. Place the sliced onion and red bell pepper in another large zip-top bag and add the remaining marinade. Seal the bag and rub to coat the vegetables. Refrigerate both bags for 2 hours. Transfer the chicken to a large Dutch oven. Discard the marinade. Add enough water to almost cover the pieces and bring to a boil over high heat. Decrease the heat to a simmer and cook for 20 minutes, or until the meat is cooked through. Line a plate with paper towels. Transfer the chicken to the plate.

In a large clean Dutch oven, heat 1 inch of vegetable oil over medium-high heat to 375°F. Set a wire rack over a rimmed baking sheet.

Working in batches, pat the chicken dry and carefully place it in the hot oil. Fry for 10 to 12 minutes, turning often, or until cooked through and juices run clear. Drain the chicken on the wire rack. Repeat with the remaining pieces.

In a heavy skillet, heat the remaining 1 tablespoon of vegetable oil until shimmering and very hot over medium-high heat. Add the marinated onion and red pepper and sauté for 3 to 4 minutes, or until beginning to soften and brown. Discard any remaining marinade.

Serve the chicken with the sautéed onions and peppers.

FILIPINO ADOBO CHICKEN THIGHS

Adobo is a popular and ingenious Philippine cooking method begun by marinating the meat, simmering it in the marinade, and then frying it until crisp. Coconut vinegar gives this authentic flavor, but apple cider vinegar also works well. You'll want to use a splatter screen and wear long sleeves for frying the coated thighs, which will erupt in a storm of popping and spewing when they hit the hot oil. If there's any sauce leftover, don't let it go to waste: use it as a dip for good bread.
SERVES 4

1¼ cups coconut vinegar or apple cider vinegar

⅓ cup soy sauce

⅓ cup chicken broth

8 cloves garlic, minced

1 tablespoon freshly ground black pepper

1 teaspoon sugar

2 bay leaves

8 skin-on, bone-in chicken thighs (about 4 pounds)

Coconut oil, for frying

Steamed rice, for serving

In a large Dutch oven, whisk together the vinegar, soy sauce, broth, garlic, pepper, sugar, and bay leaves. Add the chicken thighs and arrange so they are submerged in the mixture. Cover and refrigerate the pot for 4 hours.

Uncover the Dutch oven and bring the mixture to a boil. Decrease the heat, cover, and simmer for 30 minutes.

Line a plate with paper towels. Transfer the thighs to the plate, reserving the liquid in the pot. Increase the heat to high and simmer until the liquid is reduced to 2 cups, about 15 minutes, using a gravy separator or spoon to skim excess fat from the liquid.

In a large heavy skillet, heat coconut oil over medium heat to 350°F. It should be ½ inch deep when melted. Set a wire rack over a rimmed baking sheet.

Pat the chicken skin dry with paper towels. Carefully place the thighs in the oil, skin side down. (It will spatter like crazy.) Cover the skillet with a splatter screen and fry for 3 minutes, or until the skin is golden brown and crispy. Turn and cook for 1 minute on the second side.

Drain the chicken on the wire rack.

Serve with the reduced sauce and steamed rice.

ACKNOWLEDGMENTS

The adventure of frying several flocks of chickens has not been my journey alone. It really does take a village. My husband, Kevin; son, Camden; and daughter, Adair, ate fried chicken several times each week, sometimes several times each day, without one complaint. And they learned not to ask what was for dinner. The three of them make me happy to be alive each and every day.

My mom, Mandy Dopson, is always my saving grace, even when I'm not writing a cookbook. She did it all: running carpools, taking expert care of my children, folding clothes, and nearly everything else that chicken frying took me away from. She and my dad, William Dopson, became expert tasters and sounding boards for all things chicken.

Thank you to my sister, Natalie Schweers; my mother-in-law, Linda Lang; and my sister-in-law, Valery Hall, for cheering and encouraging me in the midst of the deepest grease.

My agent, Carole Bidnick, has been excited about this project from the moment it was mentioned. She was hands-on for every step and is an author's guiding light. I can't imagine working without her.

Thank you to the talented team at Ten Speed Press for your support and faith from the first phone call to the bookshelf. Emily Timberlake, my editor, was supportive and more than helpful. Ashley Lima, our designer; photographer John Lee; Lillian Kang, our food stylist; and prop stylist Ethel Brennan, all worked to create a beautiful book. Jean Blomquist copyedited and Erin Welke worked her magic with marketing.

Springer Mountain Farms provided all of the chickens for every aspect of this book, from meeting me on the road with fresh chickens to shipping chickens across the country. I am beyond thankful for their help and generosity. I am impressed with the way they raise and nurture their birds, and the taste is a testament to their dedication. Their vegetarian-fed chickens are 100 percent natural, given no hormones or antibiotics. They are a homegrown pride of Georgia. Kimberly Boring, Krista Beres, and everyone on the Springer Mountain Farms team at the Rountree Group were conscientious and thoughtful about keeping me in fresh chickens.

My dear friend Mark Kelly provided me with more Lodge cast-iron skillets than a girl could ever dream of. If Santa still came to see me, that's what he would bring. LouAna Foods was incredibly generous with a huge delivery of more than 25 gallons of frying oil to my back door. It fries well, and I've never found a rancid drop. Thanks to Rhonda Barlow, I had the opportunity to fry in the most beautiful skillets Le Creuset has to offer. Mary Rodgers sent me a marvelous Waring Pro deep fryer to make for the easiest chicken frying. Mary Moore, my friend, mentor, and colleague, offered the support of The Cook's Warehouse by loaning me a second Waring Pro deep fryer to further simplify my life.

My intern, Ivy Odom, was a huge help nearly every step along the way. Jennie Schacht waved her magic editing pencil over my first recipe deadline. Tamie Cook was my international fried chicken recipe researcher extraordinaire. Jeannette Dickey immersed herself in fried chicken to edit and proof my final manuscript. Dink NeSmith, a lifelong family friend, helped us set up one of the world's finest outdoor frying stations, complete with plywood and sunscreen. Downing Barber, a friend and owner of Barberitos, so kindly recycled my ocean of spent oil at his restaurant nearest my house.

Nathalie Dupree has mentored me, shared recipes, loved me, and paved my path over many years. Virginia Willis is a friend who refreshes me and is the ideal sounding board. And I am fortunate to have a group of wonderful friends and gifted colleagues who keep my culinary boat afloat, offering guidance and friendship no matter what. Jean Anderson, Gena Berry, Anne Cain, Shirley Corriher, Damon Lee Fowler, Denise Vivaldo and Sandra Gutierrez are all on that list.

Elizabeth Lamb shared her talent with the most inspirational chicken watercolors. Many others provided valuable assistance for my research, supplies, taste testing, and sanity: Gay Crowe, Karen Fooks, Meghan Garrard, Melissa and Brandt Halbach, Catherine Hardman, Philip Juras, Suzanne Kilgore, Debbie Moose, Dick Parker, Suzanne Rutledge, Lynn Sawicki, Sheila and Pat Snead, and Brooke Stortz.

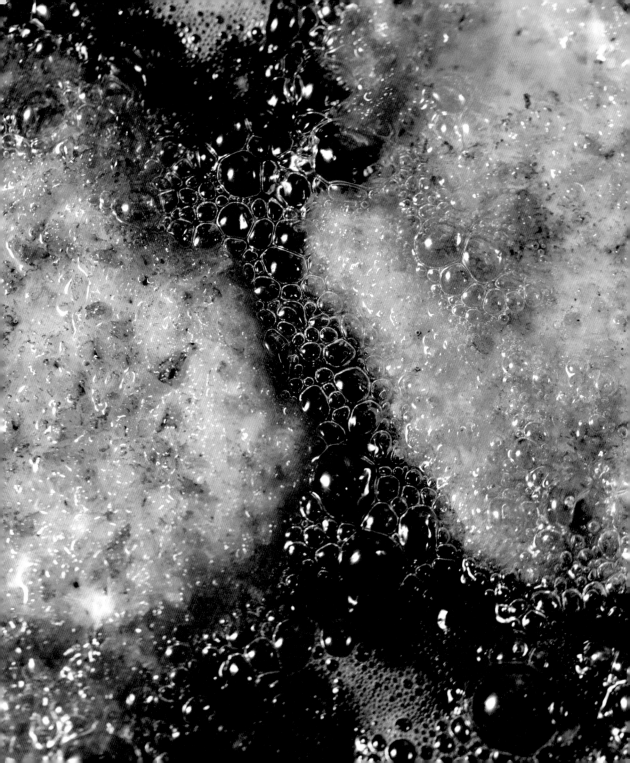

ABOUT THE AUTHOR

Rebecca Lang is a food writer, cooking instructor, television personality, and ninth-generation Southerner. Born and raised in South Georgia, she earned a culinary arts degree from Johnson & Wales University and a journalism degree from the University of Georgia. She is the author of five cookbooks. Rebecca has appeared on *Fox & Friends Weekend*, multiple segments on QVC, *WGN America's Midday News*, and numerous regional and local networks. Rebecca and her cooking have been featured in the *Wall Street Journal*, *Southern Living*, the *Atlanta Journal-Constitution*, the *Washington Post*, the *Houston Chronicle*, FoxNews.com, *Wine Enthusiast*, *Glamour*, and *Fitness*. She serves as a contributing editor for *Southern Living*, teaches cooking classes across the United States, and is a cooking expert for Ty Pennington's website. Rebecca lives in Athens, Georgia, with her husband, Kevin; their children, Camden and Adair; and their sweet Cavalier King Charles, Miss Bea.

photo by Beau Gustafson

INDEX